LEMON-AID
Self-Help

THE ART *of* COMPLAINING

CANADA'S CONSUMER ACTION GUIDE

Phil Edmonston

DUNDURN
TORONTO

Editor: Ginny Freeman Macowan
Illustrator: Rachel Rosen
Design: Kim Monteforte, WeMakeBooks.ca
Printer: Webcom

LIBRARY AND ARCHIVES CANADA CATALOGUING IN PUBLICATION

Edmonston, Louis-Philippe, 1944–, author
The art of complaining : Canada's consumer action guide / Phil Edmonston.
— 2nd edition.

Issued in print and electronic formats. ISBN 978-1-4597-1941-5 (pbk.).
ISBN 978-1-4597-1944-6 (pdf). ISBN 978-1-4597-1945-3 (epub)

1. Consumer protection—Canada. 2. Consumer education—Canada. I. Title.

HC120.C63E35 2013   381.3'40971   C2013-902968-0   C2013-902969-9

1   2   3   4   5   17   16   15   14   13

We acknowledge the support of the **Canada Council for the Arts** and the **Ontario Arts Council** for our publishing program. We also acknowledge the financial support of the **Government of Canada** through the **Canada Book Fund** and **Livres Canada Books**, and the **Government of Ontario** through the **Ontario Book Publishing Tax Credit** and the **Ontario Media Development Corporation**.

J. Kirk Howard, President

Printed and bound in Canada.

Visit us at
Dundurn.com | @dundurnpress | Facebook.com/dundurnpress
Pinterest.com/dundurnpress

Dundurn	Gazelle Book Services Limited	Dundurn
3 Church Street, Suite 500	White Cross Mills	2250 Military Road
Toronto, Ontario, Canada	High Town, Lancaster, England	Tonawanda, NY
M5E 1M2	LA1 4XS	U.S.A. 14150

Contents

INTRODUCTION

When complaints are freely heard, deeply considered and speedily reformed,
then is the utmost bound of civil liberty attained that wise men look for.

— John Milton

Canadians complain just as much as Americans, but not as well. Americans fight back hard — with small claims and class action lawsuits, with mass demonstrations, and with media manipulation. In Canada, we are, well, *Canadian*. Our grievances are politely aired and, if they are not acted upon, we vow to take our business elsewhere. Granted, sometimes we will collectively forge institutional solutions to problems (such as making healthcare available to everyone, selling our products, and protecting our culture). But individually, we tend to be pushovers.

In 2009, a Canadian survey of consumers from twenty-three countries sought to identify which population complained the most. Overall, 38 percent of participants had complained about a product or service in the past year. Brazilians were most likely to complain (65 percent); Canadians and Americans were slightly above average (44 percent); and Japanese consumers were least likely to air their grievances (17 percent).

Percentage of respondents who lodged a consumer complaint in the last year, by country:

CONSUMER COMPLAINTS					
	%		%		%
Brazil	65	Canada	44	South Korea	32
Mexico	56	Australia	40	Belgium	29
Argentina	49	Italy	39	Poland	26
India	47	France	38	Hungary	25
Czech Republic	47	Sweden	36	Turkey	22
Spain	46	Netherlands	35	Russia	18
Britain	45	Germany	34	Japan	17
U.S.	44	China	32		

Source: Ipsos Reid survey, May 2009

These findings suggest there is no difference in the percentage of dissatisfied Canadian and American consumers. The difference comes, however, in *how* we complain.

In January 2012, CBC's *Marketplace* aired a story that used a hidden camera in one Toronto store to test customers' limits with awful customer service. They found, in general, that customers were patient and unwilling to complain about the service they were getting (*www.cbc.ca/news/yourcommunity/2012/01/how-do-you-react-to-terrible-customer-service.html*).

The test demonstrated that although Canadians may be just as dissatisfied as Americans over faulty products, dangerous and unreliable automobiles, contaminated food, and unsatisfactory service, we prefer not to be seen as the squeaky wheel — at least, not overtly. As veteran *Toronto Star* consumer columnist and author Ellen Roseman pointed out, the difference is clear: "We're not big complainers; we grumble and tell our friends."

This book seeks to change all that. In the pages that follow, you will learn to see complaining in a new light:

- In Chapter 1, you will discover the many benefits of complaining, be inspired by the success stories of other complainers, and learn when complaints are justified.

- In Chapter 2, you will be introduced to your legal rights with accurate and up-to-date summaries of consumer-rights legislation and related judicial decisions.

- Chapter 3 will take you through step-by-step instructions for effective consumer complaining — enabling you to act individually to get a refund for an unsatisfactory product or service.

- The process outlined in Chapter 4 will help you to understand the benefits of collective complaining and will outline the process through which effective outcomes can be achieved.

- Chapter 5 offers a guide for using the court system as a vehicle to satisfy customer complaints, providing practical information about choosing an appropriate venue, anticipating costs, and handling the actual litigation.

- In Chapter 6, you will find specific information pertaining to complaints in the areas of vehicles, vacations, health care, and electronics.

My hope is that with all the support, encouragement, and concrete information and tips contained in this book, Canadians will feel more comfortable about standing up for their rights as consumers — in short, voicing their complaints in a way designed to reap effective results.

Chapter One

WHY COMPLAIN?

IS ANYONE TRUSTWORTHY?

Apparently, Dr. Mehmet Oz isn't — or so says the Healthy Weight Network and the National Council Against Health Fraud (*www. healthyweight.net/fraud1.html*):

> In the category of Worst Claim, our 2012 Slim Chance Award goes to Dr. Mehmet Oz who **touted raspberry ketone on** *The Dr. Oz Show* as "the number one miracle in a bottle to burn your fat." Dr. Oz claimed the product regulates the hormone adiponectin so fat in cells is "broken up" more

effectively to enable "fat burning." He declared that the product will help teach the body that it's thin. But the only relevant research cited was conducted on lab rats and mammalian cell cultures rather than clinical research on people. By the end of the show's program segment on raspberry ketone, Dr. Oz shifted into disclaimer mode arguing for the need for good diet and exercise. He then contradicted his opening miracle mongering by suggesting raspberry ketone will only "get you over the hump" and "is not a miracle pill."

But let's face it: Dr. Oz has become one of the bright stars in today's television self-help culture. And so, despite the disclaimer at the end of the segment and the critical assessments illustrated here, many consumers will have simply stopped listening after having heard Dr. Oz describe raspberry ketone as a "miracle in a bottle."

The good news, though, is that *times are changing*. Governments and the courts are becoming more responsive to consumer issues, and small claims courts are allowing claims for as much as $30,000.

On February 12, 2012, Canada's Supreme Court endorsed Quebec's "seller-beware" mindset in its *precedent-setting judgment relating to false and misleading representations* under the province's *Consumer Protection Act*. In *Richard v. Time Inc. (scc.lexum.org/decisia-scc-csc/scc-csc/scc-csc/en/7994/1/document.do)* the court held that:

- a representation should be judged simply by what a credulous and inexperienced consumer would believe to be true — a position long held by the courts in matters relating to misleading advertising charges filed under the federal *Competition Act*; and,

- if a prohibited business practice exists, there is no need to prove actual damages; an irrefutable presumption of prejudice exists (which opens the door to punitive damages, even where the circumstances do not justify a compensatory award).

Although punitive, or exemplary damages, can go as high as $1 million (see page 112: *Whiten vs. Pilot*), *Time* magazine was ordered to pay only $15,000. The impact of this award, however, has been far greater than the amount: it puts businesses and governments on notice — there's a new sheriff in town and things are going to be different.

How Do You Know When to Complain?

First, let me be clear: there are times when *you should not complain*. Contrary to the popular adage, the customer is not *always* right. Sure, we have all been spoiled by retailers who will take back a shirt or dress, no questions asked. But that is just good public relations. We don't have the *right* to a refund or exchange credit if we change our mind, paid too much, or can't find financing for the purchase. Actually, if the sale is cancelled because it can't be financed, the seller is entitled to charge a penalty to cover reasonable expenses caused by the lost sale — this is why contracts should spell out the costs that will result if they are broken.

Nonetheless, there are many times — particularly if you are faced with a defective product or an unsatisfactory service — when *you should complain.* I recommend that you claim a full or partial refund (damages) if any of the following allegations can be substantiated:

- The product is unsafe or defective; service is unsafe, inadequate, or incomplete — This principle holds true even if the product was sold "as is" or "without warranty" if the buyer can prove the seller's bad faith.

- There has been false representation or misinformation — This applies when an important characteristic of the product or service was not as represented (cost, size, warranty, performance, etc.), or important facts were not disclosed (vehicle had accident repairs, home was formerly used as a bordello, or trip insurance doesn't cover prior ailments).

- The product or service does not meet the client's needs as expressed in the contract or promised in the sales representation — For example, a no-smoking room should be just that; gluten-free meals must be gluten-free.

- The warranty has been breached — This comes into play when the guarantee wasn't honoured or differs in its application from what was promised. Since the warranty is considered to be an integral part of the contract, when it is breached (not honoured), a full or partial refund and punitive damages can be claimed from the seller, warranty company, or manufacturer. Prudent plaintiffs usually hold all parties equally responsible and let the presiding judge decide how to apportion blame.

- **Consumer-protection law is violated** — Even if the seller is contravening only a technical requirement of the law, like not giving the buyer a copy of the contract, the contract can be cancelled. In some used car cases, buyers who had paid too much were able to get their money refunded because the mileage written on the contract was incorrect or the warranty wasn't clearly stated. Judges take a dim view of standard-form contracts that aren't in conformity with the law. In fact, many consumer-protection laws require that the judge give the consumer the edge when deciding responsibility.

- **The product or service doesn't last for a reasonable period of time** — A judge has the final say as to what is a reasonable period of time; the court's decision prevails over the contract's guarantee. This rule applies to all products and services, from car repairs to tummy tucks.

- **Delivery is delayed or the price is boosted** — The seller must respect the delivery date and price given verbally or written on the contract. If there is no promised delivery date, the court will decide what is a reasonable wait based upon the industry norm.

- **Parts availability or after-sales servicing is inadequate** — There is no legal requirement that manufacturers provide parts and service beyond the warranty period. However, judges can refund part of the purchase price and award damages, even if the warranty has expired, if a product's reliability or durability is reduced due to poor servicing or an inadequate supply of replacement parts.

- **A "fix" doesn't fix the problem** — When the seller's corrective warranty repairs don't fix the problem indicated on the work order after repeated customer visits, the seller and/or manufacturer should either replace the product or pay for repairs elsewhere. If the warranty period runs out during repeated repairs, coverage for the uncorrected problem must continue until it is fixed.

- **A secret "goodwill" warranty extension isn't honoured** — Carmakers and computer manufacturers often extend their warranties long after the original warranty has expired. A problem occurs when the company applies the longer warranty in the United States only, or restricts its extension to specific regions. For example, Firestone/Bridgestone tried to limit its tire warranty extension to cars registered only in hot-weather states, until the courts showed this was impractical because cars registered elsewhere could have a catastrophic tire failure when driving through a warmer region, or after having moved to the warmer state. Incidentally, carmakers still routinely restrict their post-warranty free repairs. Fortunately, in Canada, showing a service bulletin (like the ones shown below) will usually get the free repair. (See a comprehensive listing of current secret warranty extensions in the *2014–15 Lemon-Aid New and Used Cars and Trucks* guide.)

TOYOTA CUSTOMER SERVICES

Volume: __XV__
Number: __TC08-004__
Date: __03/07/2008__
__X__ Action
__X__ Retain
____ Information

TO: ALL REGION/PRIVATE DISTRIBUTOR GENERAL MANAGERS/ VICE PRESIDENTS

FROM: DAVID CAMDEN
VICE PRESIDENT, DEALER OPERATIONS

DAVE ZELLERS
VICE PRESIDENT, PRODUCT QUALITY AND SERVICE SUPPORT

BOB WALTZ
VICE PRESIDENT, CUSTOMER SATISFACTION, TOYOTA DIVISION

SUBJECT: CUSTOMER SUPPORT PROGRAM – WARRANTY COVERAGE EXTENSION FOR FRAME RUST CORROSION PERFORATION ON CERTAIN 1995 - 2000 MY TACOMA

Toyota's secret warranty provides a valuable 15-year durability benchmark of what manufacturers should do with rust-cankered vehicles. This example should be used in negotiations with any automaker where body defects are involved.

SPECIAL COVERAGE ADJUSTMENT–CATALYTIC CONVERTER WARRANTY EXTENSION

BULLETIN NO.: 10134   DATE: NOVEMBER 17, 2010

GM

2006–07 Chevrolet Malibu equipped with 2.2L Engine (L61)
2006–07 Pontiac G6 equipped with 2.4L Engine (LE5)
CONDITION: Some customers of 2006–07 model year Chevrolet Malibu vehicles with a 2.2L engine (L61) and Pontiac G6 vehicles equipped with a 2.4L engine (LE5) may comment about the illumination of the indicator lamp. This may be due to erosion of the mat within the catalytic converter.
SPECIAL COVERAGE ADJUSTMENT: This special coverage covers the condition described for a period of 10 years or 120,000 miles (193,000 km), whichever occurs first, from the date the vehicle was originally placed in service, regardless of ownership. The repairs will be made at no charge to the customer.

Again, use this secret warranty to get a free catalytic converter replacement (it fits on the exhaust and costs about $600). Longevity is usually five years.

YOU CAN WIN: THE PERSONAL BENEFITS OF COMPLAINING

The power to make yourself heard or to right a wrong isn't something you are given. You take power from deep within your soul. Self-doubt, fear, and modesty disappear proportionally to how angry you become.

There isn't a sudden transformation from "meek, mild-mannered reporter" — it happens incrementally, over a relatively short time as indifference and lies corrode your patience and anger swells up and replaces tolerance.

Oh, the joy I have known seeing this process at work! Angry customers (soccer moms and college professors, urban and rural residents, anglophones and francophones) coming together to create their own pressure groups — the "Rusty Ford Owners Association," the "Ford Lemon Owners Group" (FLOG), the "Chrysler Lemon Owners Group" (CLOG). And then, going out to picket while holding serial press conferences, and ending up winning million-dollar settlements, all in a short span of time.

It all follows the same wonderfully effective route: communication, organization, information sharing, litigation, and legislation. Previously meek, modest, and relatively passive customers complain about a product, form a pressure group, and participate in public hearings. Strong consumer protection laws, pro-consumer court rulings, regulatory agencies (both private and public), and sustained media interest keep the issue alive.

Does this process work? You bet it does. Not only will the problem get settled, but those consumers who once felt powerless become powerful. They become advocates for justice and go on to fight for other changes. Consider the following examples:

SUCCESS STORY

Serge Pelletier knew in his gut something was wrong. He saw that his new 1973 Nissan 510 didn't have as many features as other 1973 510s. He filed suit in small claims court and won a $300 refund after Nissan admitted the cars were originally leftover 1972 models that had been "re-dated" as '73 versions.

The company claimed the auto industry (especially importers) had been rebranding leftovers for decades, and no one had complained. Automobile Protection Association lawyers countered that the cars were *originally* meant to be sold as 1972 models and didn't have the safety features that were found with "real" 1973 510s.

Nissan appealed the award to the Supreme Court of Canada. It argued that small claims courts were unconstitutional because lawyers were barred from pleading for corporations, the courts lacked jurisdiction because the proper remedy was a cancellation of the sale, and the plaintiffs didn't suffer any real damages. The Court rejected all these arguments and confirmed the $300 judgment (*Nissan v. Pelletier*, scc.lexum.org/decisia-scc-csc/scc-csc/scc-csc/en/item/5539/index.do).

The Pelletier judgment effectively shut down an industry-wide scam that had generated millions of dollars in profits from leftover cars and trucks. The appeal also confirmed the constitutionality of Quebec's small claims court system, making it impossible for other defendants to escape its jurisdiction.

SUCCESS STORY

Eric Topol is an American cardiologist and geneticist who got a dangerous drug off the market and lost his job at the Cleveland Clinic in the process.

Topol was the first physician researcher to raise questions about the cardiovascular safety of Merck's Vioxx (rofecoxib), an anti-inflammatory drug used to treat osteoarthritis and acute pain. Following Topol's criticism, the drug was voluntarily withdrawn from the market in 1994 because of concerns about the increased risk of heart attack and stroke.

It was later proven that Merck withheld information about the cardiovascular risk from doctors and patients for over five years, resulting in between 88,000 and 140,000 cases of serious heart disease. Merck had sales revenue of US$2.5 billion from Vioxx during its last year on the market.

SUCCESS STORY

Another physician known as "the guinea-pig doctor" kept his job, but made himself sick to prove the medical establishment and pharmaceutical industry wrong about the cause of stomach and intestinal ulcers.

Barry Marshall, an Australian internist and medical researcher, was so sure conventional medical wisdom was wrong about the cause of stomach ulcers that he swallowed a broth of Helicobacter pylori bacteria to prove his point. Sure enough, the brew gave him an ulcer that a regimen of antibiotics quickly and inexpensively cured.

Both Marshall and Dr. Robin Warren, a pathologist who also saw the connection between H. pylori and ulcers, had previously been dismissed worldwide as quacks by medical specialists and drug companies. After all, medical schools taught that ulcers were caused by stress and lifestyle and were best treated by drugs blocking acid production. In one bizarre study they cited, scientists gave rats ulcers by putting them in straitjackets and dropping them in ice water. Antacids were given to prevent the rats' ulcers. Based on this study, conventional treatment of patients became a lifelong diet of antacids like Tagamet and Zantac (a $3-billion-dollar industry) or removal of the stomach. Today, ulcers are easily cured with a short-term course of drugs and antibiotics, and stomach cancer, also linked to H. pylori gastritis, has been practically eradicated in the Western world.

Twenty years after their discovery was published, both doctors received the 2005 Nobel Prize for medicine.

SUCCESS STORY

Manitoba firefighter Rick Stoyko was never much of a complainer, but he needed medical help for himself and his colleagues.

He met Becky Barrett while she was going door-to-door campaigning for the provincial NDP. Stoyko had been diagnosed with brain cancer in January of 2002 and wanted Barrett's help in having cancer recognized as a work-related illness for provincial firefighters. He showed her studies of Canadian firefighters that found they were three times more likely to contract brain, bladder, and kidney cancers, as well as non-Hodgkin's lymphoma and leukemia. She agreed to take up the firefighters' cause.

Barrett won her seat and was appointed minister of labour. Shortly thereafter, she introduced Bill 5, a law making firefighters automatically eligible for workers' compensation benefits for different forms of cancer, retroactive to 1992. The law created the *presumption* that a firefighter's cancer was work-related. Under the new law, employers wishing to appeal had the burden of proof that the cancer was not work-related.

In a surprise move, the opposition Conservatives applauded the legislation, and Manitoba became the first Canadian jurisdiction with full presumptive cancer legislation. The list of cancers now presumed to be work-related injuries for full-time, part-time, or volunteer firefighters, as well as fire investigators and trainers, include breast cancer (a first in Canada), multiple myeloma, primary site prostate, and skin cancers. This brings to fourteen the number of cancers covered by presumptive legislation. The other cancers currently covered include: brain, kidney, lung, ureter, colorectal, esophageal and testicular cancers, non-Hodgkin's lymphoma, and leukemia.

Stoyko brought the media to tears during one press conference where he spoke of his love for the profession and how he hoped in his next life "to again have the honour of being a firefighter." Rick died almost ten months after the legislation was adopted. He was only fifty years old.

The health protection law for Canada's firefighters that Rick Stoyko and Labour Minister Barrett successfully championed in the Manitoba legislature has steamrolled around the world, as the following excerpt from Australia's September 2, 2011 *Senate Hansard* clearly shows. The Senate was considering a health protection bill for Australian firefighters and invited Alex Forrest, president of the United Fire Fighters of Winnipeg and Canada's representative for the International Association of Firefighters, to speak:

> It has been a great honour to be here. I would like to dedicate the work that I have done here to a firefighter from Manitoba. He was the first firefighter to be covered by occupational cancer in all of Canada. His name was Rick Stoyko. I know his family will be happy to hear that dedication. I have also reviewed the previous *Hansard* from all the people. I believe that the evidence is clear. I am not going to go into anything more because I think the position has been clear that there is a link between cancer and occupational firefighting. You have the great responsibility of putting this forward and I really look forward to the report. I also look forward to the time that I come back here and see that this legislation is passed. I want to thank each and every one of you for putting your time into this. I know politics is a thankless job sometimes, but the work that you are doing here is going to have far-reaching effect for not only Australian firefighters but around the world. I know because I am working in places such as Sweden, Finland, Israel and the UK and they are watching what is happening here in Australia right now.

The Australian bill was passed.

SUCCESS STORY

Beckie Williams combined the use of social media and a sense of humour to end U.K. retail giant Marks & Spencer's practice of adding a $10 surcharge to brassieres sized DD and up. Her campaign created a Facebook group called Busts 4 Justice in 2008. A year later, with over 18,000 members, the group forced M&S to adopt a one-price-fits-all policy. Since then, a number of independent websites have sprung up rating brassieres and retailers' practices (see *busts4justice.com/about-busts4justice/* and *www.investinyourchest.co.uk/ratings-guide*).

Marie Valée was a mom and a journalist for *Le Jour*, living in Quebec, when she became fed up with TV commercials directed at her children that pushed cereals, games, and other products. Her polite entreaties with advertisers got nowhere, so she wrote a few articles and ratcheted up the pressure. Valée founded a group of several hundred Quebecers called "Le Mouvement pour l'Abolition de la Publicité Destinée aux Enfants" and carried out a media campaign that culminated in hearings in the Quebec National Assembly and the adoption of strong laws that led to the abolition of advertising directed at children throughout Canada.

Mario Girolami is a volunteer driver who parked his truck in downtown Calgary on May 19, 2011, to deliver aid for Slave Lake fire victims. His engine was running, and he had the emergency lights on for the few moments it took to unload bedding and other items. As he was pulling away, a Calgary Parking Authority agent handed him a $315 parking ticket. Girolami called the *Calgary Sun*, showed where he had been parked, and handed out copies of the ticket. The *Sun*'s "Page Five" picked it up. The upshot? The next day the ticket was cancelled, and the two Parking Authority bosses responsible were fired over their actions.

Georges Zeliotis was a seventy-three-year old Quebec retiree who needed several hip operations and was placed on a hospital waiting list for treatment. After a year-long wait Zeliotis asked if he could pay to have hip surgery through a private health care facility and if he could buy private health care insurance. The Quebec government answered with a resounding *non*!

Zeliotis found Dr. Jacques Chaoulli, a Quebec physician who provided medical services to many of his patients at their homes. For several years, Chaoulli had been unsuccessful in getting the Quebec government to cover the costs of the home medical treatments he provided and to grant him the right to establish a private, autonomous hospital.

Patient and doctor teamed up and fought the Quebec government's refusal all the way to the Supreme Court after having their case tossed out by two lower courts. In June 2005, in a four-to-three decision, the Supreme Court ruled in favour of the plaintiffs and against the *Quebec Charter of Rights*, writing, "Access to a waiting list is not access to health care."

The successful lawsuit allows patients to be treated privately in Quebec and has opened the door to private clinics throughout Canada. Waiting lists remain but provincial healthcare facilities have to keep the waits reasonably short or pay for treatment elsewhere. Patients seeking payment for private treatment simply have to show that a long wait would unjustly deprive them of their section 7 rights under the *Canadian Charter of Rights and Freedoms*, which protects "the right to life, liberty and security of the person."

Yep, complaining works, anywhere — if it's done the right way.

WE ALL WIN: THE SOCIAL BENEFITS OF COMPLAINING

When something goes wrong, we all wonder if we really should complain. After all, we don't want to be embarrassed or proven wrong in public. Yet, somewhere deep in our soul we know that a defective product or poor service shouldn't go unheralded. We know silence is complicity, and a failure to act is cowardice. So we complain, and the world is the better for it — or, at least we feel better — for a short while, probably.

According to Professor Bryan Dwyer (*insertmarketinghere.com/tag/types-of-complainers*), complainers can be grouped into four categories:

- Passives are the least likely to complain to either the organization or to other consumers through word of mouth; they either doubt the effectiveness of complaining, or it goes against personal values and norms.

- Voicers are likely to complain to the organization but not to other consumers; they believe complaining is likely to resolve the problem.

- Irates are more likely to complain to other consumers than to the organization; unlikely to give the provider a second chance, they switch providers and actively spread negative word-of-mouth.

- Activists are the most likely to complain to the organization and to other consumers; they believe all forms of complaining have positive results.

Airing a grievance can have far-reaching consequences. In the eighteenth century, citizens' complaints over unfair taxation that were ignored by England were a big part of what led to the American Revolution and the birth of the United States.

Sometimes, the failure of government to act upon citizens' complaints can have far-reaching, unforeseen consequences that may lead to its overthrow by ballot and almost tear a country apart.

SUCCESS STORY

Former prime minister Brian Mulroney became Canada's equivalent of King George III in 1992 by turning a deaf ear to protests over his proposals to change the Canadian constitution. His inability to hear the collective grumble of the electorate sank the Charlottetown Accord in a national referendum that year. During the run-up to the vote, Prime Minister Mulroney further alienated the electorate by calling opponents of the accord "enemies of Canada." Voters complained that they were being bullied by the "political class" and rejected the accord by 54.4 percent.

A majority of voters in seven of the ten provinces (including Quebec) voted against the accord, with only Newfoundland, Prince Edward Island, New Brunswick, and the Northwest Territories voting in favour. Surprisingly, 62 percent of Aboriginals on reserves voted against the Accord as well, despite its proposals for Aboriginal self-government.

Meanwhile, Stephen Harper, a policy wonk for the conservative Reform Party, framed the referendum as the ordinary people of Canada against political "elites." In the subsequent federal election, Mulroney's Progressive Conservative Party won only two seats. The PCs were ultimately taken over by the Reform Party, and Harper is now in his third term as Conservative prime minister. In effect, a dissatisfied citizenry staged a bloodless coup — Canadian-style.

A positive consequence of the defeat of the Charlottetown Accord was the trend away from formal constitutional reform and the use of intergovernmental agreements and government legislation, like recognizing "the Québécois" as a "nation within Canada," giving Quebec veto power over future constitutional amendments, and transferring labour-market training to all provinces.

Since 1992, the phrase *constitutional reform* has become toxic in most political circles — the enduring legacy of Mr. Mulroney's bellicosity and Canada's refusal to buy a tainted product. In effect, Canadian voters did the right thing: they grumbled, and they voted.

Results of the Referendum on the Charlottetown Accord

JURISDICTION	VOTED YES	% YES	VOTED NO	% NO
Newfoundland	133,193	62.9	77,881	36.5
Prince Edward Island	48,687	73.6	17,124	25.9
Nova Scotia	218,618	48.5	230,182	51.1
New Brunswick	234,010	61.3	145,096	38.0
Quebec	1,710,117	42.4	2,232,280	55.4
Ontario	2,410,119	49.8	2,397,665	49.6
Manitoba	198,230	37.8	322,971	61.6
Saskatchewan	203,361	44.5	252,459	55.2
Alberta	483,275	39.7	731,975	60.1
British Columbia	525,188	31.7	1,126,761	68.0
Yukon	5,354	43.4	6,922	56.1
Northwest Territories	14,750	60.6	9,416	38.7
Total Canada	6,185,902	44.6	7,550,732	54.4

In the following chapters, I will help you to understand your rights as a consumer and show you winning strategies for getting a refund, respect — and maybe even revenge.

Chapter Two

2 YOUR LEGAL RIGHTS

For ordinary causes our contentious system has great merit as a means of getting at the truth. But it is a denial of justice in small causes to drive litigants to employ lawyers, and it is a shame to drive them to legal aid societies to get as a charity what the state should give as a right.

— Roscoe Pound, "The Administration of Justice in the Modern City," *Harvard Law Review*, Vol. 26 (1913), pp. 302–08

19

A Consumer Bill of Rights

In his March 15, 1962, speech to the United States Congress, President John F. Kennedy listed four basic consumer rights — to safety, to be informed, to choose, and to be heard. By 1985, the

United Nations had expanded those four into a *Consumer Bill of Rights,* which includes the right to:

- safety
- be informed
- choose
- be heard
- satisfaction of basic needs
- redress
- consumer education
- a healthy environment

Jim Guest, the President of Consumers Union and publisher of *Consumer Reports* magazine, believes there should be a ninth consumer right: the right to ***privacy***. He had this to say at the fiftieth anniversary of the Consumer Federation of America Assembly on March 12, 2012:

> Who could have predicted that we'd have a tool like the Internet that provides so much opportunity, but at the same time, exposes each and every one of us to having our most personal information put at risk? Fundamentally, when I talk about consumer privacy, I'm talking about trust. When you hand over your private information to an online company, you're trusting that your information will be treated fairly and responsibly.

Guest's warnings are particularly relevant to Canadians today. We have our own "Patriot Act," called the *Anti-Terrorism Act*, which amended the *CSIS Act* and the *National Defence Act* (read Part V.1). We have also set up our own American Foreign Intelligence Surveillance Court under the *CSIS Act*. And Canada's Communications listening is part of the "Five Eyes" international intelligence community, an alliance of five English-speaking countries that share signals intelligence.

I have my own version of a consolidated list. I believe that, basically, citizens should be:

- sold safe products,
- given the facts needed to make informed choices,
- given a reasonable number of choices at a fair price, and

- able to access an attentive government that listens and responds positively to consumer grievances and suggestions.

Today these rights are recognized and regulated through the codi-fication of civil and criminal statutes. We have thousands of laws and regulations relating to warranties, product liability, misrepre-sentation (false advertising, etc.), competition (price-fixing), and negligence and punitive damages.

Warranties

The manufacturer's or dealer's warranty is *an expressed verbal or written* undertaking that a product or service will be as represented, or the contract will be cancelled. This promise remains in force as long as the warranty hasn't expired.

The main drawback of an expressed warranty is that it allows the seller and manufacturer to act as judge and jury when deciding whether a product is defective or a service is unsatisfactory. Rarely does it provide a money-back guarantee.

Some of the more familiar lame excuses used in denying expressed warranty claims are "You abused the car"; "You spilled water on the cell phone"; "The dryer was poorly maintained"; "Bird droppings ruined your paint"; or, best of all, "It's rusting from the outside, not the inside." Or even "It passed the safety inspection." Ironically, the expressed warranty sometimes says that the goods or services are guaranteed to have no guarantee.

And, when the warranty's clauses (or lack thereof) don't deter claimants, some sellers simply say that a verbal warranty or repre-sentation as to performance or durability is unenforceable — not true. Fortunately, these attempts to weasel out of the warranty and limit the seller's liability seldom make it through judicial review.

Justice Searle put it this way in the *Chams* small claims court decision:

> Ford's warranty attempts to limit its liability to what it grants in the warranty. It is ancient law that one who attempts to limit his liability by, for example, excluding common law remedies, must clearly bring that limitation to the attention of the person who might lose those remedies. The evidence in this case is clear: The buyer of even a new car does not get

a warranty booklet until after purchasing the car although he "would be" told the highlights sooner (*2013 Lemon-Aid New Cars and Trucks* guide, pp.136–42).

Thankfully, car owners get another kick at the can with the implied warranty — this is the promise of "fitness." In the unreported Saskatchewan decision *Maureen Frank v. General Motors of Canada Limited* (see chapter 6), the judge declared that paint discoloration and peeling shouldn't occur within eleven years of the purchase of a vehicle. Both of the above-cited judgments leave no doubt that *the implied warranty usually trumps an expressed restriction.*

The implied warranty is solidly supported by a large body of federal and provincial laws, regulations, and jurisprudence, and it protects you primarily from hidden dealer- or factory-related defects. But the concept also includes misrepresentation and a host of other scams.

This is a powerful "super" warranty that sellers never tell you about. It also holds businesses to a higher standard of conduct than private sellers because, unlike private sellers, professionals are presumed to be aware of the defects present in the products they sell. That way, they can't just pass the ball to the manufacturer and then walk away from the dispute.

The *implied warranty* is so effective with cars and other goods because it:

- is always in effect and cannot be abrogated by a bad faith clause in the contract like "sold, as is, without warranty";

- is frequently used by small claims court judges to give refunds to plaintiffs "in equity" (out of fairness) rather than through a strict interpretation of contract law;

- establishes the concept of "reasonable durability," meaning that parts are expected to last for a reasonable period of time as stated in jurisprudence, judged by independent experts, or expressed in extended warranties given by the manufacturer in the past through "goodwill" warranty extensions;

- covers the entire product and can be applied for whatever period of time the judge decides;

- can require that the product be taken back, or that a major repair cost be refunded;

- can help plaintiffs claim compensation for extra expenses incurred because of a product's failure, including inconvenience, mental distress, missed work, lodging, and ruined vacations — as well as exemplary (or punitive) damages in cases where the seller behaved particularly badly;

- applies during and after the expiration of the manufacturer's or dealer's expressed or written warranty and requires that a part or repair will last a "reasonable" period of time.

Product Liability

Judges usually apply the implied or legal warranty when *there's no expressed warranty, or when the manufacturing defects remain uncorrected*. Notably, two landmark judicial decisions uphold implied warranties in Canada, one relative to drinks served in a bar and the other concerning car quality. Additionally, our courts have been active in applying the implied warranty in everything from electronic goods to botched vacations, the habitability of rented apartments, home and condo purchases, the safety of blood transfusions, and whether a bar association can be held responsible for a careless act when no malice is intended. This last case shows that the concept of "product liability" applies not only within the realm of products but also when it comes to services.

Let's first take a look at the *Finney v. Barreau du Quebec* decision rendered in 2004, in which the Supreme Court awarded an aggrieved client of a member of the Barreau (bar) $25,000, plus solicitor and client costs, for "moral damages" because her lawyer failed to prosecute diligently and had a history of serious professional misconduct. What makes this case unique is that it proves lawyers aren't above the law when their work is sub-standard. This was the first time that a professional regulatory body was found liable for failing to protect the public. As the Court noted, "The delegation of [regulatory] powers by the State imposes obligations on the governing bodies of the profession, which are then responsible for ensuring the competence and honesty of their members in their dealings with the public."

The Court ruled the Barreau could not escape liability by pleading good faith in the performance of its duties: "It would be contrary to the fundamental objective of protecting the public if this immunity were interpreted as requiring evidence of malice or intent to harm to rebut the presumption of good faith. Gross or serious carelessness is incompatible with good faith."

This judgment was a shot across the bow of all self-regulated professions and should help ensure they act in a timely manner to discipline members who don't provide what they promise, whether they are doctors, lawyers, or accountants.

In *Donoghue v. Stevenson*, [1932] A.C. 562 (H.L.), the court had to determine if the manufacturer of a bottle of ginger beer owed a duty to a consumer who suffered injury as a result of finding a decomposed snail in the bottle after consuming part of the bottle's contents. Lord Atkin, in finding liability against the manufacturer, established the principle of negligence. His reasons have been followed and adopted in all the common-law countries:

> The rule that you are to love your neighbour becomes in law, you must not injure your neighbour; and the lawyer's question, who is my neighbour? receives a restricted reply. You must take reasonable care to avoid acts or omissions which you can reasonably foresee would be likely to injure your neighbour. Who, then, is my neighbour?
>
> The answer seems to be persons who are so closely and directly affected by my act that I ought reasonably to have them in contemplation as being so affected when I am directing my mind to the acts or omissions which are called in question.

More than three decades ago, the Supreme Court of Canada clearly affirmed, in *General Motors Products of Canada Ltd. v. Kravitz*, [1979] 1 S.C.R. 790, that automakers and their dealers are jointly liable for the replacement or repair of a vehicle if independent testimony shows that it is afflicted with factory-related defects which compromise its safety or performance.

The existence of secret warranty extensions or technical service bulletins also help prove that a product's deficiencies are the manufacturer's responsibility. For example, in *Lowe v. Fairview Chrysler* in 1989, technical service bulletins were instrumental in showing that Chrysler had a history of automatic transmission failures similar to what we see in Ford and GM vehicles today. In addition to replacing or repairing the product, the seller and manufacturer can also be held responsible for any damages arising from the defect (see the case summary referring to *Wharton*, Chapter 5). This means that loss of wages, supplementary transportation costs, and damages for personal inconvenience can be awarded.

When a warranty claim is rejected on the pretext that the customer "altered", failed to carry out preventive maintenance on, or damaged the product, manufacturers *must* prove to the court that there's a link between their allegation and the failure (see *Julien v. General Motors of Canada Ltd.* [1991], 116 N.B.R. [2d] 80).

Misrepresentation

Misrepresentation or false advertising is illegal under federal and provincial laws and carries both civil and criminal penalties. Under the *Competition Act*, federal authorities regularly get multi-million dollar settlements from businesses that stretch the truth — or simply lie — to their customers. And, it doesn't take much to start the ball rolling: a simple on-line denunciation (at *www.competitionbureau.gc.ca/eic/site/cb-bc.nsf/frm-eng/GH%C3%89T-7TDNA5*) will suffice to start an investigation that could cost a company millions.

As can be seen in the federal court ruling against Bell Canada, Ottawa's position is similar to Quebec's: if qualifying information is necessary to prevent a representation from being false or misleading when read on its own, then that information should be presented clearly and conspicuously. "Fine print" won't do.

CASE SUMMARY

Bell Canada found this out the hard way on June 28, 2011, when it consented to pay a $10 million settlement (the first time that the maximum penalty for misleading advertising has ever been imposed) and change its advertising after the Canadian Competition Bureau said the ads were contrary to the *Competition Act's* civil prohibition against making representations that are false or misleading.

Bell made false, misleading representations for over five years about the prices at which certain of its services were available (including home phones, Internet, satellite television, and wireless services). Bell's representations gave the "general impression" that the advertised monthly price for the services was sufficient, when in fact Bell used a variety of "fine-print disclaimers" to "hide" additional mandatory fees which made the actual price paid by consumers higher than the advertised price (in one instance 15 percent higher than advertised). According to the *Competition Act's* misleading advertising provisions, the "general impression" conveyed by the advertisement to the average consumer, as well as its literal meaning, were considered in determining that the representations made were false or misleading. The settlement between Bell and the Bureau is set out in a "consent agreement" found at *www.ct-tc.gc.ca.*

As with most businesses caught scamming the public, Bell maintained it did no wrong. Nevertheless, the company paid the $10 million fine and agreed to drop all non-compliant advertising within sixty days. In particular, Bell agreed not to use small print or other ancillary disclosures that contradict the general impression of its price representations. Bell also agreed to pay the Competition Bureau $100,000 to cover the costs of [the Bureau's] investigation.

Abuse of Trust

Abuse of trust is a polite way of saying to someone in authority "you lied." Such a breach need not be intentional or malicious, but can be due to negligence, as was likely the case with Texaco and the Alberta Motor Association, below.

CASE SUMMARY

We are the Men from Texaco
We wear the Texaco Star
We like to think at Texaco
We've got everything for your car
We've got wipers for your windshield
Plugs 'n' belts 'n' tires, too
Lubricants and batteries and polishes for you
All the things to keep your engine up to par
We've got everything for your car
That's why you can trust you car to the man who wears the Star
for the finest products that can take care of you car
At every Texaco station, clean across the nation
You can trust your car to the man who wears the Star
The big, bright Texaco Star!

In 1961, Texaco came up with the above jingle, which not only was hugely successful in promoting the company's products but also won lawsuits for motorists who say they were ripped off by Texaco gas station repairs. Apparently, Texaco's ad created a higher expectation of trust and that trust was abused by its franchisees. The jingle also figured in a $170 million racial discrimination lawsuit filed by black employees and settled by the company. It was the largest racial discrimination lawsuit settlement in the United States at the time, and was particularly damaging to Texaco's public relations when tapes were released containing alleged ethnic slurs used repeatedly by company officers at high-level corporate meetings. The officers insisted they did not use the N-word, but were only referring to one of the black employees, "Nicholas."

Over the years the company had also been accused of damaging the environment, cheating its franchisees, and overpricing its products. In 1987 Texaco filed for bankruptcy.

CASE SUMMARY

Davies v. Alberta Motor Association (August 13, 1991; Alberta Provincial Court, Civil Division; No. P9090106097; Judge Moore): The plaintiff had a used 1985 Nissan Pulsar NX checked out by the AMA's Vehicle Inspection Service prior to buying it. The car passed with flying colours. A month later, the clutch was replaced, and then numerous electrical problems ensued. At that time, another garage discovered that the car had been involved in a major accident, had a bent frame and a leaking radiator, and was unsafe to drive. The court awarded the plaintiff $1,578.40 plus three years of interest. The judge held that the AMA set itself out as an expert that was trusted by the plaintiff and should have spotted the car's defects. The AMA's defence — that it was not responsible for errors — was thrown out. The court held that a disclaimer clause could not protect the association from a fundamental breach of contract.

Lafont v. Alberta Motor Association (May 3, 2011; Alberta Court of Queen's Bench; [2011] A.J. No. 513; 2011 ABQB 305; Judge Manderschied): After a fire destroyed the insured's home, the Alberta Motor Association Insurance Company refused the claim because the claimant was no longer a member of the automobile association, which meant the insurance policy wasn't automatically renewed. The insured argued that this wasn't specified in his policy. The court agreed. The policyholder was entitled to coverage under the policy because membership was not a condition precedent to coverage and it was a reasonable assumption the policy would be renewed annually.

American Express (AMEX) was the first company to create a large-scale traveller's cheque system in 1891, and is still the largest issuer of traveller's cheques. It has made millions in profits because purchasers of its cheques trust that they will get reimbursed right away if the cheques are lost or stolen. Unfortunately, American Express also stretches the truth in its ads promising an "immediate" reimbursement.

For example, in the early 1970s I vacationed in Panama where I had served as a U. S. Army medic a decade earlier. I bought US$1,000 worth of American Express traveller's cheques in Montreal. Halfway through my vacation, the cheques were stolen and I asked AMEX to replace them. They were replaced a week later; the vacation had been ruined.

Back in Canada, I sent a claim to American Express for $300 — Quebec's small claims court limit. I explained that their service was not as advertised (an "immediate" refund) and that I would file a claim in one week with the Quebec small claims court if I was not compensated for my loss of time and inconvenience. Within the week, a cheque for $300 arrived by courier.

Did AMEX learn its lesson? I don't think so. When I Googled American Express while researching this book, I came across other recent cases where customers were not immediately paid the money that was lost or stolen on vacation.

One angry customer wrote this about his experience with AMEX traveller's cheques (*www.consumeraffairs.com/credit_cards/amex_travelers_cheques.html*):

> $1,350 in traveller's cheques was stolen from me during a trip to Thailand. I notified American Express as well as the local police. The police took the report and gave me signed a statement regarding the theft. On the American Express website they write that, "Your money is always safe with traveller's cheques", and just below that they add that if your money is lost or stolen, it will usually be refunded within 24 hours. I was sure that all it would take would be a few phone calls, faxes, and I would get my money back safely just like American Express claims.
>
> The nightmare began when I called American Express to report the stolen traveller's cheques. Right off, the representative told me that I would probably not get my money back within 24 hours as the website claims, and that I should try to find another way to get money (I was stuck with just $100 in Thailand). They said it would likely be a long process. In the subsequent months,

I found myself having countless discussions with customer representatives, sending dozens of emails along with photocopied documents, bank account statements, my lease agreement (to prove where I live), and answering dozens of questions that included my height and weight and many other extraneous details.

If I had just lost $50 or $100, I might have given up, as I'm sure many people do, but the amount stolen from me was so great that I kept trying. I kept up with calling, e-mailing, photocopies, faxes, and everything else. After months of this process, I finally received a letter from American Express stating that they refused to give me back my money even though the cheques were cancelled and cannot be used. They claimed there is insufficient substantiation that any cheques were lost/stolen. In addition, they now claim that all further communication with them must be conducted through written documents only, so basically calling them does me no good. One word describes the customer service at American Express: indifference.

Competition

In 2014, the *Competition Act* is expected to be used in addressing issues such as:

- beer distribution in Ontario,

- advertising pharmacy dispensing fees, and

- a code of conduct for wireless service providers to address clarity and content in service agreements. Specifically, Ottawa seeks to discourage "switching costs," which reduce customer mobility, and wants consumers to receive better information that would enable them to make wise choices. These actions are meant to create greater competition in wireless markets, leading to lower prices, higher quality service, and greater innovation.

The *Competition Act* also has scored a notable victory in stamping out the age-old "Yellow Pages" business scam that sent bogus subscription bills to businesses via unsolicited faxes. Under this act, Ontario's Court of Appeal upheld a $500,000 penalty (the statutory maximum for an individual is $750,000) against the defendant in the case, noting that the scammers had used fictitious advertising companies to net many millions of dollars with very low costs.

Until the *Competition Act* was applied by the Competition Bureau, the individuals involved had blatantly disregarded orders from the Ontario Superior Court to stop defrauding businesses through the phony invoice scheme.

Negligence and Punitive Damages

Negligence is defined by the courts as the failure to use reasonable care, resulting in harm to another party. Either a person does something that a reasonable person would not do, or fails to take action that a reasonable person would take to prevent harm. Punitive damages (also known as "exemplary damages") allow plaintiffs to obtain compensation that exceeds his or her quantifiable losses; this acts as a deterrent to those who would carry out dishonest or negligent practices.

Judgments involving punitive damages, common in the United States, sometimes reach hundreds of millions of dollars. Canadian courts, however, have seldom awarded substantial punitive damages. There have been a few relatively recent cases where the Supreme Court of Canada has shocked the business establishment by levying huge exemplary damage awards.

CASE SUMMARY

One such case was the *Whiten v. Pilot Insurance Co.* decision rendered in 2002. In this case, the plaintiff's home caught fire and burned to the ground, destroying all of the home's contents and killing three pet cats. Pilot Insurance made a single $5,000 payment for living expenses and covered the family's rent for a couple of months, and then cut off the rent payments without forewarning the family. The insurance claim went to trial, on the basis of the respondent's allegation that the family had torched their own home, even though the local fire chief, the respondent's own expert investigator, and its initial expert all said there was no evidence whatsoever of arson. The original trial jury awarded the plaintiff compensatory damages and $1 million in punitive damages. Pilot Insurance fought this decision at the Court of Appeal, where the punitive damages award was reduced to $100,000. The case was then taken all the way to the Supreme Court, where the trial jury's unprecedented award of $1 million was restored:

> The jury's award of punitive damages, though high, was within rational limits. The respondent insurer's conduct towards the appellant was exceptionally reprehensible. It forced her to put

at risk her only remaining asset (the $345,000 insurance claim) plus $320,000 in costs that she did not have. The denial of the claim was designed to force her to make an unfair settlement for less than she was entitled to. The conduct was planned and deliberate and continued for over two years, while the financial situation of the appellant grew increasingly desperate. The jury evidently believed that the respondent knew from the outset that its arson defence was contrived and unsustainable. Insurance contracts are sold by the insurance industry and purchased by members of the public for peace of mind. The more devastating the loss, the more the insured may be at the financial mercy of the insurer, and the more difficult it may be to challenge a wrongful refusal to pay the claim.

CASE SUMMARY

Time magazine also ended up paying punitive damages for its high-handed conduct that violated Quebec's misleading advertising laws in much the same way as Bell Canada's ads violated the *Competition Act* and earned that company a $10 million fine. In *Richard v. Time Inc.* (*scc.lexum.org/decisia-scc-csc/scc-csc/scc-csc/en/item/7994/index.do*), the Supreme Court reduced the plaintiff's punitive damages awarded to the plaintiff, Jean-Marc Richard, from $100,000 to $15,000. According to the judgment,

> In his mail, R received an "Official Sweepstakes Notification" (the "Document") in the form of a letter supposedly signed by the manager responsible for the sweepstakes. Along the edge of the letter were boxes printed in colour, some of which, because they referred to *Time* magazine, could lead the recipient to infer that it was from T and TCM [Time Inc. and Time Consumer Marketing Inc.].
>
> In the Document, which was written in English only, several exclamatory sentences in bold uppercase letters, whose purpose was to catch the reader's attention by suggesting that he or she had won a cash prize of US$833,337, were combined with conditional clauses in smaller print, some of which began with the words "If you have and return the Grand Prize winning entry in time". In addition, the back side of the letter informed R that he would qualify for a $100,000 bonus prize if he validated his entry within five days. The mailing also contained a reply coupon and

a return envelope on which the official rules of the sweepstakes appeared in small print. The reply coupon also offered R the possibility of subscribing to *Time* magazine. As well, the rules stated that a winning number had been pre-selected by computer and that the holder of that number could receive the grand prize only if the reply coupon was returned by the deadline. If the holder of the pre-selected winning number did not return the reply coupon, the rules explained, the grand prize winner would be selected by random drawing among all eligible entries, that is, everyone who had returned the reply coupon, and each participant's odds of winning would then be 1:120 million. Convinced that he was about to receive the promised amount, R immediately returned the reply coupon that was in the envelope. In doing so, he also subscribed to *Time* magazine. R began regularly receiving issues of the magazine a short time later, but the cheque he was expecting was a long time coming. He contacted T and TCM, which informed him that he would not be receiving a cheque, because the Document had not contained the winning entry for the draw and was merely an invitation to participate in a sweepstakes. They also informed him that the manager who had signed the letter did not exist; the name was merely a "pen name".

R filed a motion to institute proceedings in which he asked the Quebec Superior Court to declare him to be the winner of the cash prize mentioned in the Document and to order T and TCM to pay compensatory and punitive damages corresponding to the value of the grand prize. The Superior Court allowed the action in part. It held that the Document contravened Title II of the *Consumer Protection Act ("C.P.A.")* on prohibited business practices and that the civil sanctions provided for in s. *272 C.P.A.* were accordingly available. The judge set the value of the moral injuries suffered by R at $1,000 and fixed the quantum of punitive damages that were also awarded to him at $15,000.

In particular, punitive damages are rarely awarded in Canadian courts against automakers. When they are given out, it's usually for sums less than $100,000. In *Prebushewski v. Dodge City Auto (1985) Ltd. and Chrysler Canada Ltd.*, the plaintiff was awarded a mere $25,000 in a judgment handed down in 2001 and confirmed by the Supreme Court in 2005. This despite the extreme fact scenario: the plaintiff's 1996 Dodge Ram's running lights had shorted and caused her truck to burn to the ground, and Chrysler had refused her claim. In granting the punitive damages, the court basically said that, under provincial consumer protection statutes, aggrieved car owners may sue for much more than the depreciated value of what they bought. The Supreme Court also reaffirmed the power of the lower courts to assess an additional financial penalty to punish automakers that treat their customers unfairly and thus ensure they don't repeat the offence.

In *Vlchek v. Koshel* (1988; 44 C.C.L.T. 314, B.C.S.C., No. B842974), the plaintiff was seriously injured when she was thrown from a Honda all-terrain cycle, on which she had been riding as a passenger. The court allowed for punitive damages because the manufacturer was well aware of the injuries likely to be caused by the cycle. Specifically, the court ruled that there is no rigid legal principle stipulating that punitive or exemplary damages can only be granted if the defendant's acts were specifically directed against the plaintiff. The court may apply punitive damages "where the defendant's conduct has been indiscriminate of focus, but reckless or malicious in its character. Intent to injure the plaintiff need not be present, so long as intent to do the injurious act can be shown."

For more examples of awards for exemplary damages, see:

- *Granek v. Reiter* (Ontario Court, General Division; No. 35/741);

- *Morrison v. Sharp* (Ontario Court, General Division; No. 43/548);

- *Schryvers v. Richport Ford Sales* (May 18, 1993; B.C.S.C., No. C917060; Judge Tysoe); and,

- *Varleg v. Angeloni* (B.C.S.C., No. 41/301).

Most provincial business practices legislation covers false, misleading, or deceptive representations and allows for punitive damages should the unfair practice toward the consumer amount to an unconscionable representation (see *Canadian Encyclopedic Digest [C.E.D.]*, Third Edition, s. 76, pages 140–45). Here are some specific cases to keep in mind:

- Exemplary damages are justified where compensatory damages are insufficient to deter and punish. See *Walker et al. v. CFTO Ltd. et al.* (1978; 59 O.R. [2nd], No. 104; Ontario C.A.).

- Exemplary damages can be awarded in cases where the defendant's conduct was "cavalier." See *Ronald Elwyn Lister Ltd. et al. v. Dayton Tire Canada Ltd.* (1985; 52 O.R. [2nd], No. 89; Ontario C.A.).

- The primary purpose of exemplary damages is to prevent the defendant and all others from doing similar wrongs. See *Fleming v. Spracklin* (1921).

- Disregard of the public's interest, lack of preventive measures, and a callous attitude all merit exemplary damages. See *Coughlin v. Kuntz* (1989; 2 C.C.L.T. [2nd]; B.C.C.A.).

- Punitive damages can be awarded for mental distress. See *Ribeiro v. Canadian Imperial Bank of Commerce* (1992; Ontario Reports 13 [3rd]) and *Brown v. Waterloo Regional Board of Commissioners of Police* (1992; 37 O.R. [2nd]).

Defamation and Libel

Picketing a clinic, hospital, business office, or factory, having a "sit-in" at the local auto show, or placing an ad rounding up other "lemon" owners are all legitimate public-interest complaint tactics that get results — and, sometimes, arrests and lawsuits. However, the legal intimidation hanging over these actions is now a past threat thanks to the Supreme Court's intervention.

In December 2009, the Court rendered two judgments that make it much harder for plaintiff businesses to win cases alleging defamation or libel. The first decision overturned a lower court award of $1.5 million to a forestry executive who sued the *Toronto Star*. The *Star* alleged that he had used political connections to get approval for a golf course expansion (see *Grant v. Torstar Corp.*).

The Supreme Court struck down the judgment against the newspaper because it had failed to give adequate weight to the value of freedom of expression. ***The court announced a new defense of "responsible communication on matters of public interest."*** In the court's opinion, anyone (journalists, bloggers, unions, picketers, etc.) can avoid liability if they can show that the information they communicated — whether true or false — was of public interest and they tried their best to verify it.

In another case, also involving a major Canadian newspaper, a former Ontario police officer sued the *Ottawa Citizen* after it reported that he had misrepresented his search-and-rescue work at Ground Zero in New York City after the attacks of September 11, 2001. The Supreme Court quashed his $100,000 jury award because the judges felt the article was in the public interest (see *Quan v. Cusson*).

Chapter Three

HOW TO GET YOUR MONEY BACK

So, you've purchased a product or service that just isn't satisfactory. But, unlike the majority of Canadians, you've learned that grumbling to your friends is not going to resolve your problem. You're determined to register a complaint — but you're not entirely sure how to go about it.

Fear not. By working through this five-step process, you will become an effective complainer. And — unless you find yourself embroiled in a major class-action lawsuit — you are most likely going to be successful in getting your money back.

STEP 1: START WITH INFORMAL NEGOTIATIONS

Try to settle things informally with a phone call, even knowing that this tactic rarely works. Customer service agents (who recite policies but don't make them) may simply say that the warranty doesn't apply or that it is the store's policy not to give refunds. This brush-off usually convinces 90 percent of complainers to drop their claims after some angry venting.

Nevertheless, *don't take no for an answer.* Contact someone higher up who has the authority to bend policies to satisfy your request. Speak in a calm, polite manner, and try not to polarize the issue. Talk about cooperating to solve the problem. Let a compromise emerge —don't come in with a hard set of demands.

For example, *find out what it would cost to have the product replaced or fixed by an independent company that agrees your complaint is valid.* Giving the seller this information will show that you have a serious claim and the facts needed to win your case in court. Use the independent repair estimate to challenge the seller's offer to pay half the repair costs (too often, sellers will then try to jack up the price 100 percent so that you wind up paying the whole shot!)

Don't insist on getting the settlement offer in writing, but make sure that you're accompanied by a friend or relative who can confirm the offer in court if it isn't honoured. Be prepared to act upon the offer without delay so that if the other party withdraws it, they won't be able to blame your hesitancy.

STEP 2: ESCALATE TO A FORMAL, WRITTEN COMPLAINT

Don't worry; no one feels comfortable writing a complaint. But *if you haven't sent a written claim letter, fax, or email, you haven't really complained* — or at least that's the mindset of most corporations. Here are a few basic tips for how to go about it.

If a new or used car is involved, send *both the dealer and the manufacturer* a polite registered letter, fax, or email that asks for compensation for repairs that have been done or need to be done. Include insurance costs during the vehicle's repair, towing charges, supplementary transportation costs like taxis and rented cars, and damages for your inconvenience.

Don't shy away from being graphic and creative. If the apartment is overrun by cockroaches, rats, and the like, send photographs. Give one of the varmints an alliterative pet name ("Rover" the Roach? Roscoe the Rat? Mickey or Minnie Mouse?) and send the landlord pictures and greeting cards for Father's/Mother's Day, Minnie's Baby Shower or any other celebratory occasion. Use email as you set up Rover's Twitter, Facebook, and website accounts and be sure to copy local media. Keep any evidence — such as invoices, guarantees, or receipts — separate from your primary letter, but attach them by paper-clipping them on the back. *And remember, always send photocopies, not originals, in case your correspondence gets lost in the mail.*

Addressing a letter to the legal department or to the General Counsel's office at a large company routes the letter directly to a lawyer who will have the power to meet your demands. Mark "Enclosure" on the envelope so the recipient will know there is more material in the package. *Don't* threaten anyone or call names. *Do* calmly state you will use small claims court within a certain time period if there is no satisfactory resolution of your grievance.

Specify five days (but allow ten days) for either party to respond. If no satisfactory offer is made or your claim is ignored, file suit in small claims court. Make the manufacturer a party to the lawsuit, especially if a safety-related recall campaign, an emissions warranty, a secret warranty extension, or an injury or death is involved (see the following sample complaint letters).

STEP 3: GET THE GOVERNMENT INVOLVED

As a former member of Parliament, I can assure you: a complaint letter copied to your local MP brings results. Manufacturer representatives want to lobby the government with a "clean slate" and to stay "on message." The last thing they want is an MP shoving unresolved owner complaints under their nose at some committee hearing. Another advantage in getting a government official involved is that MP offices have paid staff who know whom to contact in both government and industry to apply extra pressure to get your problem resolved.

STEP 4: TRY MEDIATION OR ARBITRATION

If the formality of a courtroom puts you off, or you're not sure that your claim is all that solid and don't want to pay the legal costs to find out, *consider using mediation or arbitration* offered by these groups: the Better Business Bureau (BBB), the Automobile Protection Association (APA), the Canadian Automobile Association (CAA), small claims court (mediation is often a prerequisite to going to trial), provincial and territorial government–run consumer mediation services, and the Canadian Motor Vehicle Arbitration Plan (CAMVAP). In all the above cases, arbitration is voluntary. With sales contracts, the binding arbitration requirement can be dropped, if all parties agree.

Binding arbitration is a poor substitute for consumer-friendly small claims court litigation, yet an increasing number of sales contracts contain mandatory binding arbitration provisions that force the buyer to use independent arbiters to settle disputes. Businesses favour this process because it's relatively inexpensive, decisions are rendered more quickly than through regular litigation, there is a less formalistic approach to the rules of evidence, jurisprudence isn't created, and the process is less public than an open courtroom trial.

The disadvantages to binding arbitration are many and include: loss of recourse to the courts, no appeals, no jurisprudence to guide plaintiffs as to the rules of law used in prior decisions (which often leads to quicker settlements or encourages litigants to stand by their principles), and the chumminess that often develops between arbiters and serial defendants, who may meet often over similar issues throughout the year, thus creating a familiarity that breeds contempt — for justice that is.

The most serious drawback of arbitration is that the other side can refuse to take back the product or pay the cost of repairs simply by arguing that the arbitration process was flawed because the arbitrator exceeded his or her mandate.

I don't want to give the impression that binding arbitration is a useless tool for obtaining redress. For example, CAMVAP has worked fairly well with some new car disputes. On the other hand, it proved woefully ineffective in resolving the "death wobble" on Dennis Warren's 2007 Dodge Ram 2500 (see *www.cbc.ca/m/touch/ news/story/2011/05/16/bc-dodgeproblem.html*).

Binding arbitration agreements are also a convenient way for manufacturers to hide design or production defects that are carried over year after year, since plaintiffs must file their cases individually and cannot pool their resources.

CASE SUMMARY

CAMVAP is the best-known organization offering free arbitration to new car owners in Canada (1-800-207-0685; *www.camvap.ca*).

Though CAMVAP presents its arbitration program as a free, fast, and fair process, some plaintiffs who have used CAMVAP's system say that the arbitration awards aren't enforced, multiple hearings may unduly delay a final judgment, and there is an undue reliance upon successive repair attempts before a final settlement is achieved. Three recent cases come to mind:

- The owner of a Ford Focus found paint abraded to the bare metal along the side of his doors. CAMVAP's arbitrator said it was a design flaw and ordered the vehicle repainted. Ford appealed the judgment. After a year, Ford's case was thrown out of court. Ford may appeal to the next higher court and the Focus owner may have to wait another two years and hire a lawyer.

- Ford again. An F-150 was running badly. CAMVAP's arbitrator initially said the powertrain was fine. He later revised his decision and Ford refused to accept his change of heart.

- The Chrysler Ram had what is commonly referred to as a "death wobble" whenever the truck passed over potholes or uneven terrain (no kidding — check out "Dodge Ram death wobble" through Google). Chrysler refused to take back the vehicle as ordered by the CAMVAP arbitrator. The truck's owner contacted the CBC and the vehicle was recalled.

STEP 5: EXPOSE THE PROBLEM USING THE INTERNET AND OTHER MEDIA

Use the Internet, particularly social media sites, to call attention to your problem and/or seek advice. You might want to post an entry in an appropriate forum describing your plight and ask for information from people who may have experienced a similar problem. This approach alerts others to the potential problem, helps build a base for a class action or a group meeting, and puts pressure on the other party to settle. Groups can form quickly through Twitter and other social media.

Television producers and their researchers need articulate consumers with issues that are easily filmed and understood. If you want media coverage, you must summarize your complaint and have visual aids that will hold viewers' interest (viewers should be able to understand the issues with the sound turned off).

Some tactics you may use that have been successful:

- Use email to send JPEG pictures of bad home repairs, a dirty hotel room, or a paint-delaminated car.

- Give the seller a "Lemon" prize and accompany it with a press release.

- Give your group a nifty name like FLOG, CLOG, "Mr. Badwrench," or "Vacationers from Hell."

- Create a website that clearly sets out your goals and lists people to contact.

- Call a press conference in front of the agency with which you are in disagreement, and find a way to visually show what is wrong. Hand out a summary of your grievance with supporting documents that tell the story. Carry a sign that can be easily read ten to twenty feet away, decorate your vehicle, or show an injury.

- Be polite but firm, and don't interfere with traffic or annoy shoppers. All you want is to meet with someone responsible to review the issue and perhaps reconsider their earlier decision.

This approach works with government functionaries just as well as it does with business owners and professionals. It's the intensity of the story coupled with your reasonableness and some film or pictures showing your displeasure that will get the story on the afternoon radio news and the 6 p.m. TV news, and in the next morning's newspaper — which may be picked up again by the open-line radio shows for another day.

You can have fun and put additional pressure on a seller or garage by putting a "lemon" sign on your car and parking it in front of the dealer or garage, by creating a "lemon" website, or by forming a self-help group like the Chrysler Lemon Owners Group (CLOG) or the Ford Lemon Owners Group (FLOG). After forming your group, you can have the occasional parade of creatively decorated cars visit area dealerships as the local media are convened. Just remember to keep your remarks pithy and factual, don't interfere with traffic or customers, and remain peaceful.

One other piece of advice from this consumer advocate with more than forty years of experience and hundreds of pickets and mass demonstrations under his belt: *Keep a sense of humour, and never break off negotiations.*

Finally, don't be scared off by threats that it's illegal to criticize a product or company. Unions, environmentalists, and consumer groups do it regularly (it's called "informational picketing"), and the Supreme Court of Canada in *R. v. Guinard* reaffirmed this right in February 2002.

CASE SUMMARY

In that judgment, an insurance policyholder posted a sign on his barn claiming that the Commerce Insurance Company was unfairly refusing his claim. The municipality of Saint-Hyacinthe, Quebec, told him to take the sign down. He refused, maintaining that he had the right to state his opinion. The Supreme Court agreed. This judgment means that consumer protests, signs, and websites that criticize the actions of corporations cannot be banned simply because they say unpleasant things.

Chapter Four

HOW TO COMPLAIN SUCCESSFULLY

YOU HAVE JUST WON $1 MILLION DOLLARS,
IF YOU SUBSCRIBE TO TIME...HOLD YOUR BREATH FOR FIVE
MINUTES, SING ALL STANZAS OF "O'CANADA" IN BOTH
LANGUAGES, AND TELL US WHERE SENATOR MIKE DUFFY LIVES.

As an individual or as part of a collective — and regardless of whether you're looking for compensation or for a policy change within a corporation or government — you need to follow the same five strategic steps to achieve a successful outcome.

STEP 1: COMMUNICATE

Begin by doing your homework: communicate with others to establish a base for your claim. *Contact experts* to confirm that a product or service is not satisfactory. Then carefully *review all of the sales literature relative to your warranty rights* and how the product should perform.

Then *find out if others have had a similar experience.* Use the Internet to see if others have been dissatisfied or filed suit against the company, government agency, or service provider. This can be done by using the Google search engine and typing in "complaints", "problems," or "defects" after the product's name or agency's title. Professionals, such as doctors and lawyers, can be further checked out by adding "misconduct" or "malpractice" to a Google search. If you want to see if a company or individual has sued or been sued in civil court, insert the name followed by *v.*, or *v.* then the name. If there was a criminal case, put an *r* before or after the *v.* You can also find others who have had similar experiences through Twitter and other social media.

STEP 2: ORGANIZE

If everything validates your claim, *create a "paper trail"* by sending a claim letter, email, or fax to the seller or service provider. Politely ask for a refund or a change of policy and allow at least a week for a response.

If you are invited to a meeting to discuss the problem, be sure to *bring a relative or friend along* to keep you focused and to serve as a witness.

Don't rush negotiations. If remedial action is promised, make sure everyone agrees to what is offered and the timeline.

STEP 3: INFORM THE GOVERNMENT

If there is no satisfactory response, *contact the media and register your complaint with the provincial government's consumer affairs ministry.* Ontario, for example, has a unique way of alerting businesses to your complaint by forwarding it with the government's own covering letter.

Ontario's sly bureaucrats do say they haven't initiated a *formal* investigation, yet — they are just passing on a consumer's complaint.

Ministry of Consumer Services

Consumer Protection Branch
Place Nouveau
5775 Yonge St. Suite 1500
Toronto ON M7A 2E5
Telephone: 416-326-8800
Facsimile: 416-326-8665

Ministère des Services aux consommateurs

Direction de la protection du consommateur
Place Nouveau
5775 Yonge rue. bureau 1500
Toronto ON M7A 2E5
Téléphone: 416-326-8800
Télécopieur: 416-326-8665

Notification of a Consumer Complaint

You are receiving this document because a customer has a complaint about your business and believes you have contravened the Consumer Protection Act, 2002 (CPA). At this time, the Ministry of Consumer Services (Ministry) has not initiated a formal investigation into this complaint.

The Consumer Protection Branch (CPB) of the Ministry administers and enforces a number of consumer protection laws. The CPB monitors the Ontario consumer environment to ensure fairness and ethical conduct by businesses.

It is Ministry policy that consumers who have a complaint write a letter to the business to see if they can resolve the problem. A letter from your customer is attached.

Please take a moment to consider the details of the attached letter. You may also wish to review your obligations under the *Consumer Protection Act, 2002*. Your efforts to resolve the matter described in the letter may avoid the need for the Ministry to become involved. Our objective is to ensure that consumers and businesses have information about their rights and obligations that is clear and easy to understand.

If you have not responded to the issue outlined in the attached letter within three weeks, the consumer may file a formal written complaint about your business with the Ministry. If the issue outlined in the complaint falls under the CPA, the Ministry may step in to help mediate a solution between you and the consumer. If the ministry is unable to mediate a solution, or your business is found to be in contravention of the CPA, the Ministry may choose to take compliance action against you or your business.

Where a Ministry investigation finds a violation of the CPA has occurred, charges may be laid. Successful prosecution under the CPA may result in fines of up to $50,000 for an individual or imprisonment for a term of not more than two years less a day or both and, if convicted, a corporation may be liable to a fine of not more than $250,000.

Under the CPA, the Ministry of Consumer Services is required to post information about businesses who fail to respond to consumer complaints; actions it has taken against a business; and charges laid and convictions.

This information is posted on Ontario's Consumer Beware List at Ontario.ca/consumerbeware – an online searchable public record. Where information relating to a charge(s) is posted on the public record, the business is not guilty of an offence, unless so determined by a court of law. The information appearing in the public record is current as of the date of printing.

You are welcome to contact our office, toll free at 1-800-889-9768 or at (416) 326-8800 for more information about the *Consumer Protection Act, 2002* and your responsibility to consumers.

But, what is most likely to stick in the letter recipient's mind is this paragraph:

> Where a Ministry investigation finds a violation of the CPA has occurred, charges may be laid. Successful prosecution under the CPA may result in fines of up to $50,000 for an individual or imprisonment for a term of not more than two years less a day or both and, if convicted, a corporation may be liable to a fine of not more than $250,000.

Ottawa will go one step further. Its online form solicits citizen reports of dishonest business practices. One such complaint forced Toyota to settle a price-fixing investigation by giving $2 million to a Canadian charity, and another resulted in General Motors Canada paying a $20,000 fine after lying about its Firenza reliability.

Government investigators treat all information as confidential and look into allegations of price-fixing, misleading advertising, false weights and measures readings (such as car odometers), and a host of other prohibited activities — as described by the *Competition Act*, the *Consumer Packaging and Labelling Act*, the *Textile Labelling Act*, and the *Precious Metals Marking Act*. Such complaints are administered by the Competition Bureau (see *www.competitionbureau.gc.ca/ eic/site/cb-bc.nsf/frm-eng/GH%C3%89T-7TDNA5*).

But *what if you are ticked off about poor government service?* Well, the federal government has a bilingual free website for that, too. No kidding, it's called Service Canada (*www.servicecanada.gc.ca/ eng/ocs*).

STEP 4: LITIGATE

After several weeks, *file a claim in small claims court*. Use the original complaint letter and attach the sales contract, proof of defect (an evaluation from an independent expert will do), and an estimate for corrective repairs (same expert's report).

STEP 5: LEGISLATE

Legislative action should follow if the courts claim you or your group lack standing, the court doesn't have jurisdiction, or the defendant is judgment-proof. The fuss kicked up by an unsuccessful lawsuit creates considerable momentum to change the law so other scams are prevented or future claimants will get their money back. This is how class actions got their start in Canada's provincial legislatures. The Supreme Court threw out the Firenza collective-action suit on the grounds that a collective action could not be used as a substitute for a class action. Therefore, the courts lacked jurisdiction. This ruling forced the provinces to step in with their own class-action laws.

Chapter Five

HOW TO NAVIGATE THE LEGAL SYSTEM

Going to regular court should be the last resort. Your spirit will get stomped, and your wallet will get walloped. H. Patrick Glenn, in his article "Costs and Fees in Common Law Canada and Quebec," says litigants are running away from high-cost courts and lawyers *(www-personal.umich.edu/~purzel/national_reports/Canada.pdf).*

If, however, you find yourself in a situation that demands legal action, begin by familiarizing yourself with the information provided below.

Parties are allowed to represent themselves in Canadian courts; counsel is generally required only in cases of representation of a corporate body or a person with a disability (see, for example, *CCP, art.61, Ont. RCP 7*). With today's high costs of litigation, this has indeed become a frequent occurrence. It is estimated that almost 30 percent of cases now involve self-representing parties. The rising incidence of self-representation has in fact become a concern of the judiciary, given the adversarial nature of proceedings. Up to 95 percent of cases are settled out of court to avoid legal costs.

How Expensive is it to Go to Court?

The June 2009 issue of *The Canadian Lawyer* published a summary of average legal fees within Canada. From the following highlights of that article (*www-personal.umich.edu/~purzel/national_reports/Canada.pdf*), it is easy to see how difficult it would be for many Canadians to pay to have their "day in court":

• The average hourly fee for an Ontario lawyer with ten years experience was $382 — though some fees were as high as $900 per hour.

• The hourly fee for lawyers in the western provinces was $467.

• In Quebec, 2 percent of the profession was charging more than $500 per hour, with a further 1 percent at more than $400 (*Le Journal du Barreau du Québec*, May 2009).

• In Ontario, legal fees for a one-party, two-day trial would range from $18,738 to $90,404.

• The average cost (in Ontario) to each party in a two-day dispute would be $45,477.

Not surprisingly, litigants are fighting back by shunning lawyers and representing themselves, making contingency fee arrangements, asking for pay-as-you-go court costs, and searching out small claims courts where filing fees barely top $200 and lawyers are optional, if not barred entirely.

Contingency-Fee Lawyers

If you are too poor to afford legal counsel but earn too much for legal aid, consider hiring a lawyer on a contingency-fee basis, and go through the regular court system. In Canada contingency fees vary from 20 to 45 percent of the proceeds awarded, and the client pays nothing unless and until there is recovery in the lawsuit. This fee arrangement particularly suits plaintiffs with wrongful dismissal and serious injury claims who likely have little income.

All contingency fee agreements are subject to court review; however, the agreement you signed in the lawyer's office will carry a lot of weight as to your intentions. Note, however that *many contingency-fee agreements provide that although there is no legal fee payable if the case is lost, the client remains responsible for reimbursing the lawyer for disbursements paid out.*

There are many ways to structure a contingency fee agreement that is fair to both client and lawyer. For example, one could *provide for a percentage fee that decreases (or increases) depending on the level of financial recovery. In some Canadian personal injury and medical malpractice matters, a higher percentage is due on the first $100,000 awarded and a lower percentage on compensation recovered in excess of $100,000.* The contingency-fee percentage should apply to recovery less any costs awards.

Another way to avoid excessive up-front legal costs is to ask the court to make provisional or interim costs orders as a means of financing the suit. This may be granted where the plaintiff cannot afford the litigation, appears to have a meritorious claim, and raises issues of public importance (*British Columbia [Minister of Forests] v. Okanagan Indian Band [2003] 43 C.P.C. [5th] 1*).

Beware the "Court Costs" Surprise

Although filing fees are quite low, going from $20 (Saskatchewan) to $218 (Quebec), additional "court costs" may be added at the end of the trial. In Ontario, for example, a successful litigant's disbursements may be charged to the losing party. These can include costs of effecting service; expenses for travel, accommodation, and photocopying; witness expenses; and experts' reports. An unsuccessful party may also have to pay a self-represented successful party an amount not exceeding $500 as compensation for inconvenience and expense. If a successful party is represented by a lawyer, student-at-law, or agent, the court may award the winning side a reasonable representation fee at trial or at an assessment hearing.

A calm, respectful demeanour in court may save you some court costs, however. Although an award of costs in small claims court, other than disbursements, should not exceed 15 percent of the amount claimed, the presiding judge may increase the costs to penalize a party or a party's representative for unreasonable behaviour during the proceeding.

USING THE COURTS

It is well known that disputes that go before the courts can last a very long time. The plaintiff may face interminable delays setting and postponing hearing dates; long, drawn-out hearings; procedural roadblocks; appeals; and long-awaited judgments. For example, in the judicial district of Montreal, the period between filing a legal claim and the hearing date is fourteen to fifteen months. In 2006, British Columbia's small claims division registered a median period of 296 days from filing a legal claim to the hearing date.

When to Sue

If the other party you've been negotiating with agrees to make things right, set a deadline for compensation, repairs, or a replacement. Have an independent expert verify that repairs have been done adequately. *If no offer is made within ten working days, file suit in court.* Make the manufacturer a party to the lawsuit if the original, unexpired warranty is still in place, or if the product wasn't reasonably durable or of "merchantable quality." With a disputed service, sue only if a regulatory body is dragging its feet, then make it a co-defendant under the *Finney* doctrine. Also, make sure you have solid independent experts showing the service wasn't acceptable.

Which Court?

It all depends upon how much money you want and how much you can spend to get it. Sure, it's nice to sue on principle, but a cash award makes that principle more apparent and gives you back some of what you lost. It makes no sense, however, to spend $50,000 in legal costs over a $35,000 dispute. This is why small claims courts are so attractive.

Whether you are suing over an unsatisfactory service or a faulty, or misrepresented product, small claims court, with a top limit of $30,000, keeps court fees at a minimum and is by far the most efficient court in which to have a dispute settled.

Small claims courts are on the lowest rung of the provincial or territorial court system. Then there is Superior Court, a Court of Appeal, and finally the Supreme Court of Canada. Each court can hear civil or criminal trials. Each court level can increase legal costs and delay the final judgment exponentially (expect a two-year wait at each level after small claims court).

SMALL CLAIMS COURTS

These popular, informal "people" courts can't award million-dollar judgments, but neither do they take forever to decide a case or bankrupt litigants with excessive legal fees. Fortunately, businesses usually settle disputes through pre-trial mediation or at a settlement conference because their time and costs often far outweigh what would be gained — never mind the bad publicity arising from court filings and eventual judgment. Other disincentives for defendants include the fact that small claims courts can award sizable sums to plaintiffs not represented by lawyers, and they often create jurisprudence that other judges on the same bench are likely to follow.

Indeed, small claims court judges take their court work very seriously — even though they are sometimes wild characters. Maybe it's the informality of the courtroom, or the court's mandate to rule what is fair (equitable), rather than applying broader, more technical legal rules, such as rules of evidence or hearsay. Or, perhaps it's because they see more cases in a week than most judges see in a month. But after sitting through hundreds of small claims cases for four decades as a *pro bono* expert witness, I have gained tremendous respect for these common-sense judges who give soothing counsel to nervous claimants, castigate witnesses who perjure themselves, and render judgments that are unassailable.

CASE SUMMARY

For example, in *Dawe v. Courtesy Chrysler* (Dartmouth Nova Scotia Small Claims Court; SCCH #206825; July 30, 2004), Judge Patrick L Casey, QC, rendered an impressive twenty-one-page decision citing key automobile product liability cases from the past eighty years, including *Donoghue*, *Kravitz*, and *Davis*. The court awarded $5,037 to the owner of a new 2001 Cummins engine-equipped Ram pickup with the following problems: it wandered all over the road; lost power or jerked and bucked; shifted erratically;

lost braking ability; bottomed out when passing over bumps; allowed water to leak into the cab; produced a burnt-wire and oil smell in the interior as the lights would dim; and produced a rear-end whine and wind noise around the doors and under the dash. Dawe had sold the vehicle and reduced his claim to meet the small claims threshold. Anyone with water leaking into the interior or problems with the engine, transmission, or suspension will find this judgment particularly useful.

"Small claims" court is quickly becoming a misnomer. New Brunswick claimants can sue up to a maximum of $30,000, and most other courts allow claims that vary from $20,000 to $25,000, with Quebec bringing up the rear at $7,000.

There are small claims courts in most counties of every province where one can easily fill out a Statement of Claim. Or you can download the same form online and have it processed in the area where the problem happened or where the defendant lives and conducts business. Remember, you must identify the defendant correctly, which may require some help from the court clerk. Try looking for other recent lawsuits naming the same party; crooks often change their company's name to escape liability. For example, it would be impossible to sue Joe's Supermarket (1999) if your contract is with Joe's Supermarket, Inc. (1984).

Before You Go to Court

It wouldn't hurt to *visit the courthouse and attend a morning of small claims trials*, especially if your claim will be presented unassisted or if a large amount of money is involved. A paralegal or lawyer can be also be hired for a brief walk-through of small claims procedures to ensure that you've prepared your case properly and that you know what objections will likely be raised by the other side. If, instead, you'd like a lawyer to do all the work for you, there are a number of law firms around the country that specialize in small claims litigation. "Small claims" doesn't necessarily mean "small legal fees," however, although some law offices charge a flat fee of $500–$1,000 for a basic small claims lawsuit and trial.

Keep in mind that tips in this guide are not meant as legal advice. Everything should be checked out by a paralegal or lawyer intern.

Paralegals and lawyer interns are good sources of support. Paralegals usually have lots of small claims experience, are familiar with the paperwork, cost far less than a lawyer — and are likely to return your phone calls. Lawyer interns want to prove they are good advocates. Their law school-fresh idealism and enthusiasm to see justice prevail is invaluable. Plus their fees are quite reasonable. All these factors easily compensate for an intern's lack of experience. Again, small claims work is mostly procedural, not rocket science.

Court clerks, family, friends, or co-workers are excellent sources for referring good legal help. Alternatively, you can get referrals from community organizations, university legal assistance, consumer groups, and provincial law societies, like the Law Society of Upper Canada (*www.lsuc.on.ca*).

Small Claims Limits Across Canada

See the following maximum claims table, and check your provincial or territorial court's website for specific rules and restrictions. Also, save time by downloading claim forms and other documents from the Internet (Google "small claims court Ontario," for example).

CLAIM LIMITS FOR SMALL-CLAIMS COURTS IN CANADA			
Province	**Claim Maximum**	**Province**	**Claim Maximum**
Alberta	$25,000	Nunavut	$20,000
British Columbia	$25,000	Ontario	$25,000
Manitoba	$10,000	Prince Edward Island	$8,000
New Brunswick	$30,000	Quebec	$7,000
Nova Scotia	$25,000	Saskatchewan	$20,000
Northwest Territories	$10,000	Yukon	$25,000

It is also important to note the following information:

- Plaintiffs with claims exceeding the maximum allowed may abandon the excess portion.

- Disputes involving title to land, slander, libel, bankruptcy, false imprisonment, or malicious prosecution must be handled in a superior court.

- In Quebec, people who appear before the Small Claims Division represent themselves, without a lawyer, and appeals are limited.

Remember that you're entitled to bring to court any evidence relevant to your case, including written documents such as contracts, letters, or bills of sale or receipts. If your car has developed severe rust problems, bring a photograph (signed and dated by the photographer) to court. You may also have witnesses testify in court. It's important to discuss a witness's testimony prior to the court date. If a witness can't attend the court date, he or she can write a report and sign it for representation in court. This situation usually applies to an expert witness, such as an independent mechanic who has evaluated your car's problems.

If you lose your case in spite of all your preparation and research, some small claims court statutes allow cases to be retried in exceptional circumstances, at a nominal cost. If a new witness has come forward, additional evidence has been discovered, or previously unavailable key documents have become accessible, apply for a retrial.

Justice Marvin A. Zuker's *Ontario Small Claims Court Practice 2013* (Carswell, 2012) serves as an excellent reference full of tips on filing, pleading, and collecting a judgment. Judge Zuker's annual publication is easily understood by non-lawyers and uses court decisions from across Canada to help you plead your case successfully in almost any Canadian court.

Reasonable Diligence

Whatever reason you use to get your money back, *don't forget to conform to the "reasonable diligence" rule that requires you to file suit within a reasonable time after the item's purchase or after you've discovered the defect.* In the case of car problems, if there have been no negotiations with the dealer or automaker, this period shouldn't exceed a year. If either the dealer or the automaker has been promising to correct the defects for some time, or has carried out repeated unsuccessful repairs, the delay for filing the lawsuit can be extended from the time negotiations ended.

Trial Tactics

It's essential that printed evidence and/or witnesses (relatives are not excluded) be available to confirm that a false representation actually occurred, that a part is failure-prone, or that its replacement is covered by a secret warranty. Stung by an increasing number of small claims court defeats, automakers are now asking small claims court judges to disallow evidence from *Lemon-Aid*, service bulletins, or memos on the pretext that such evidence is hearsay (not proven) unless confirmed by an independent mechanic or unless the document is recognized by the automaker's or dealer's representative at trial. It is always a good idea to bring in an independent garage mechanic or body expert to buttress your allegations. Sometimes, though, the service manager or company representative will make key admissions if questioned closely by you, a court mediator, or the trial judge. That questioning can be particularly effective if you call for the exclusion of witnesses until they're called (let them mill around outside the courtroom wondering what their colleagues have said).

Automakers often blame owners for having pushed their vehicle beyond its limits. Therefore, when you seek to set aside the contract or get a repair reimbursed, it's essential that you get the testimony of an independent mechanic and his or her co-workers in order to prove that the vehicle's poor performance isn't caused by negligent maintenance or abusive driving.

Legal Phrases You Should Know

When using Canadian courts, it's a good idea to be trilingual, with a good knowledge of English, French, and Legalese. The following phrases are ones that you are mostly likely to encounter when filing or pleading a lawsuit:

- Audi alteram partem (Hear the other side). This is most often used to refer to the principle that no person should be judged without a fair hearing in which each party is given the opportunity to respond to the evidence against him or her.

- Caveat emptor (Let the buyer beware). Purchasers are responsible for checking whether goods suit their needs. This concept ruled the consumer protection movement until the publication of Ralph Nader's *Unsafe at Any Speed* in the sixties. That book, which exposed the design deficiencies of GM's Corvair, argued that more effective legislation was needed to force a "seller-beware" mindset. British Columbia, Saskatchewan, and Quebec were the first provinces to apply this doctrine in legislation relative to automobile warranties and the interpretation of what is reasonable durability.

- Ex post facto law (From after the action). A law that retroactively changes the legal consequences (or status) of actions committed or relationships that existed prior to the enactment of the law.

- Ignorantia juris non excusat (Ignorance of the law excuses no one). A legal principle holding that a person who is unaware of a law may not escape responsibility for violating that law.

- Pro bono publico (For the public good). The term is generally used to describe professional work undertaken voluntarily and without payment as a public service.

- Mens rea (A guilty mind). This goes to the defendant's intent, and is considered one of the necessary elements of a crime.

- Quanti minoris (A reduced amount, or diminished value). A partial refund may be claimed based upon the reduced value of a product due to the manufacturer's or seller's negligence or misrepresentation. This principle was used successfully against Nissan and Ford of Canada by the Automobile Protection Association in hundreds of small claims court cases during the seventies. Refunds of up to $300 were awarded as compensation to buyers who were sold "redated" new vehicles that were the previous year's model. Nissan appealed the awards to the Supreme Court of Canada, claiming small claims courts were unconstitutional because lawyers were barred from pleading. A second argument was that the small claims courts lacked jurisdiction because the proper remedy was a cancellation of the sale. This would have taken the cases out of the courts' $300 maximum jurisdiction. The Supreme Court rejected both arguments (see *Nissan v. Pelletier*).

- Ratio decidendi (The point in a case which determines the judgment, or the principle which the case establishes).

- Res ipsa loquitur (The thing speaks for itself). The elements of duty of care and breach can be sometimes inferred from the very nature of an accident or other outcome, even without direct evidence of how any defendant behaved.

- Restitutio in integrum (Restoration to the original condition). This is one of the primary guiding principles behind the awarding of damages in common law negligence claims. The general rule, as the principle implies, is that the amount of compensation awarded should put the successful plaintiff in the position he or she would have been in had the wrongful action not been committed. Thus, the plaintiff should clearly be awarded damages for direct expenses, such as medical bills and property repairs, and the loss of future earnings attributable to the injury (which often involves difficult speculation about future career and promotion prospects). This is also a term used to describe how far insurance companies must go in repairing accident damage.

Reasonable Durability

From sixty-inch plasma-screen TVs to $89,000 Tesla electric sports cars, Canadian law says that what we buy must be of merchantable quality, perform as represented, and be reasonably durable. If not, the buyer can choose to have it fixed or replaced and get a little change on the side for the inconvenience.

The reasonable durability claim is your ace in the hole. It's probably the easiest allegation to prove, since all manufacturers have benchmarks as to how long body components, trim and finish, and mechanical and electronic parts should last. For an automobile, the "reasonably durable" standard depends on the price paid, the kilometres driven, the purchaser's driving habits, and how well the vehicle was maintained by the owner. With that plasma-screened fancy TV, it may mean how much Pepsi got into the control console. Judges carefully weigh all these factors in awarding compensation or cancelling a sale.

How do you know when a part or service doesn't last as long as it should, and whether you should seek a full or partial refund? Sure, you have a gut feeling based on your use of the vehicle, how you maintained it, and the extent of work that was carried out on it. But you'll need more than emotion to win compensation from garages and automakers.

You can definitely get a refund if a repair or part lasts longer than its guarantee but not as long as is generally expected. But you'll have to show what the auto industry considers to be "reasonable durability." Automakers, mechanics, and the courts all have their own benchmarks as to what constitutes a reasonable period of time or amount of mileage one should expect a part or adjustment to last. Consequently, I've prepared a chart (see Appendix B) to show what most automakers consider to be reasonable durability, as expressed by their original and "goodwill" warranties.

Refunds for Other Expenses

It's a lot easier to get reimbursed for a defective part or poor service than it is to obtain compensation for a missed day of work.

Manufacturers seldom pay for consequential expenses like a ruined vacation, a vehicle not living up to its advertised hype, or an owner's mental distress, because they can't control the amount of the refund. Courts, however, are more generous, having ruled that all expenses (damages) flowing from a problem covered by a warranty or service bulletin are the manufacturer's or dealer's responsibility under both common law (which covers all provinces except Quebec) and Quebec civil law. Fortunately, when legal action is threatened — usually through small claims court — automakers quickly up their ante to include most of the owner's expenses, because they know the courts will probably do the same.

CASE SUMMARY

One precedent-setting judgment which gave generous damages to a motorist fed up with his "lemon" Cadillac was rendered in 1999 by the British Columbia Supreme Court in *Wharton v. Tom Harris Chevrolet Oldsmobile Cadillac Ltd.* ([2002] B.C.J. No. 233, 2002 BCCA 78d). In that case, Justice Leggatt threw the book at GM and the dealer in awarding the following additional amounts:

(a) Hotel accommodations: $217.17

(b) Travel to effect repairs at 30 cents per kilometre: The plaintiff claims some 26 visits from his home in Ucluelet to Nanaimo. Some credit should be granted to the defendants since routine trips would have been required in any event. Therefore, the plaintiff is entitled to be compensated for mileage for 17 trips (approximately 400 km from Ucluelet to Nanaimo return) at 30 cents per kilometre.
$2,040.00
TOTAL: $2,257.17

[20] The plaintiffs are entitled to non-pecuniary damages for loss of enjoyment of their luxury vehicle and for inconvenience in the sum of $5,000.

Chapter Six

ISSUES YOU MAY WANT TO COMPLAIN ABOUT

In previous chapters, I've laid out the general framework for launching a consumer complaint: the who, what, when, where, why, and how. Now we're going to get more specific and look at some of the more common situations in which consumers find themselves unsatisfied with a product or service and are motivated to take action by complaining.

Cell Phones

Apple has reportedly agreed to a $53 million settlement in a class-action lawsuit alleging breach of contract, common-law fraud, and unjust enrichment. The suit targets defective iPhones and iPods: owners of the iPhone, iPhone 3G, iPhone 3GS, and the first three generations of the iPod Touch were refused warranty-related repairs and replacements. Owners will likely get refunds of between $200 and $500, although the maximum award could be 200 percent of the phone's original price. Lawyers may get up to 30 percent of the settlement.

Why would Apple automatically deny warranty service to so many loyal customers? Apparently because the company mistakenly thought the phones had been dunked in water if a white indicator tape embedded in the phone near the headphone or charging portals had turned pink or red. Apple later learned from 3M, which manufactured the tape, that humidity could have caused the tape to turn pink. (See Apple's "Stipulation of Settlement," in *re Apple iPhone/iPod Warranty Litigation*; Case No. CV-10-1610, April 10, 2013.)

Televisions

An LG Electronics class action lawsuit seeks to represent anyone who purchased certain defective LG televisions that failed prematurely. These include but are not limited to models 32LC2D, 37LC2D, 42LC2D, 42PC3D, 42PC3DV, 47LC7DF, and 50PC3D.

The lawsuit alleges that the televisions use printed circuit boards that prematurely fail during the normal operation of the television. The defect is present at delivery and ultimately results in the failure of the televisions themselves well before the end of their expected useful life.

Consumer Reports' recent ground turkey lab-analysis found over half of its samples tested positive for fecal bacteria. No wonder that one in six Americans becomes ill from bacterial infections after eating contaminated food. Most of them fully recover after a few days of discomfort. Nevertheless, about 130,000 are hospitalized and 3,000 die. In Canada, it is estimated that more than 400,000 people suffer food poisoning every year without even realizing it.

Bad food in Canada has a long history. The Quebec Inquiry into Organized Crime found that tainted food intended to be sold as pet food found its way into hot dogs and hamburgers sold at Montreal's 1967 world exposition. But even though the diseased meat racket was public knowledge, health inspectors took bribes to look the other way and government officials who suspected what was going on did nothing.

Food contaminated by foreign substances or objects is a relatively rare occurrence, and runs the gamut from toxic chemicals through slivers of glass in a bottle of Pepsi-Cola to dead mice found in butter and flour.

What about finding a mouse in your Molson? Unlikely, and there is no evidence of it happening in Canada.

The McKenzie brothers, played by Rick Moranis and Dave Thomas, used "a mouse in the beer bottle" as a running gag in *Strange Brew*, a 1983 Canadian comedy film. In the film, two unemployed brothers, Bob and Doug McKenzie, place a live mouse in a beer bottle in an attempt to blackmail the local beer store into giving them free Elsinore beer. At the brewery, the brothers are given jobs on the bottling line inspecting the bottles for mice.

Missouri judge Randy Anglen *did* find a dead mouse in his beer bottle. On a Tuesday in May 2004, Anglen came home from work, had dinner, and grabbed a Miller Lite from the fridge. He drained the last bit into the sink so he could put the bottle in his recycling bin.

Then he saw the dead mouse in the bottle.

The next morning, a Miller representative told him to pack the bottle in dry ice and mail it to them so "they could determine if it was a mouse," Anglen said. "The first thing I said was, 'I'm an attorney, and that's the evidence.'" The representative told Anglen that it might be a clump of algae in the bottle.

"I've never seen algae with four little feet and a tail and a head and grey fur," Anglen said. There's no word whether the judge was given a free case of beer for his trouble.

A decomposed snail in a bottle of ginger beer in England forever changed the common law doctrine of negligence used in Canada. *Donoghue v. Stevenson* [1932] is a foundational case for English tort law. It set out general principles whereby one person would owe another person a duty of care.

Also known as the "snail in the bottle" case, the facts involved Mrs. Donoghue drinking a bottle of ginger beer in a café. A snail was in the bottle. She fell ill, and she sued the ginger beer manufacturer,

Mr. Stevenson. The House of Lords held that the manufacturer owed a duty of care to her, which was breached, because it was reasonably foreseeable that failure to ensure the product's safety would lead to harm to consumers.

CASE SUMMARY

Lemay v. La Ferme St-Laurent (October 17, 1975, Quebec Superior Court, No. 500-05-005996-72): A dead mouse was found in a pound of butter. Plaintiff was awarded $2,300 for mental distress and her husband got $200 for out-of-pocket expenses.

Curll v. Robin Hood Multifoods, Ltd. (56 D.L.R. [3d], 129): Plaintiff found a dead mouse in a bag of flour. Court awarded the plaintiff $500 for her mental distress, plus $13 for the bag of flour.

Smith v. Pepsi Cola of Canada Ltd. (December 14, 1967, Supreme Court of Ontario): Plaintiff had slivers of glass stick in her throat and mouth after drinking a bottle of Pepsi-Cola. She received $5,400 in damages.

Mcneil v. Airport Hotel Halifax Ltd. (September 22, 1980, Nova Scotia Supreme Court): The plaintiff fell sick after eating poultry that was insufficiently thawed and undercooked. The court awarded plaintiff $4,100.

Heimier v. Calvert Caterers Ltd. ([1974], 8 O.R. [2nd], 1 [Ont. C.A.]). Guests at a catered wedding reception contracted typhoid fever spread by one of the caterers. The catering firm was held liable for damages.

HEALTH CARE ISSUES

Health Products Misrepresented

Expiration dates on packages of common over-the-counter drugs are fraudulent and used as marketing tools, according to three separate fraud class-action lawsuits filed recently.

The lawsuits seek actual and punitive damages from Pfizer (Advil), Bayer (Bayer Aspirin) and Johnson & Johnson (Tylenol Cold Multi-Symptom medications). Plaintiffs say the drug makers use "unconscionable, unfair, deceptive, unethical and illegal" means to promote the sales of their products. This involves using expiration dates that aren't relevant to the efficacy of the drug.

The class-action cites studies by the Food and Drug Administration, Harvard Medical School, and Johns Hopkins University that have found 90 percent of more than 100 prescription and over-the-counter drugs were fine and could be used for as much as fifteen years after their expiration dates: this excludes certain drugs like tetracycline, nitroglycerin, insulin, and liquid antibiotics.

Medical Malpractice

To win a medical malpractice lawsuit you need to prove you were harmed by a doctor's mistake and be ready for a long, expensive battle. Even then, the odds are against you — more so in Canada than in the United States.

For example, of 894 Canadian malpractice lawsuits resolved in 2011, 293 were settled out of court, while 533 were dismissed, abandoned, or discontinued. Of the few that actually made it to trial, plaintiffs won in only thirteen of sixty-eight cases.

The Canadian Medical Protective Association (CMPA) is a little-known non-profit organization that provides malpractice insurance to doctors and acts much like a trade union safeguarding their welfare in civil court for medical negligence, and in criminal trials for crimes ranging from over-billing to felony assault. Even administrative matters like doctors regaining their hospital privileges or over-billing aren't too small for the CMPA's heavy legal artillery.

So what's wrong with doctors having a union to promote their interests and fight patients' lawsuits? Plenty. They're using our money to fight us, says the patient advocacy website *www.tuum-est.com*:

> In 2004 the CMPA signed a sweetheart deal with the provinces to allow CMPA insurance premiums to be subsidized by taxpayer money. Each province has its own rebate program, and subsidies range from 80 to 100 percent. Ontario, for instance, pays 90 percent of the $49,000 in annual fees CMPA charges obstetricians. The CMPA fought to keep arrangement with the provinces confidential, but a successful Freedom of Information application brought it out in the open in 2008.

More telling is how the CMPA uses its $2.7 billion taxpayer-funded war chest to grind down litigants through costly procedures, delays, and discoveries. Two relatively recent Ontario Superior Court decisions are highly critical of the association's tactics in the courtroom. These two cases show exactly what kind of defence you can expect from the CMPA and how to tailor your Statement of Claim so it is accepted by the court. Although the plaintiffs won both lawsuits, the trials were gruelling. No wonder few malpractice cases make it to trial.

CASE SUMMARY

Ornstein v. Starr (2011 ONSC 4220 [CanLII], November 29, 2011; *canlii.ca/t/ fp3mf*): Presiding Master D.E. Short wrote, "When the surgical note candidly and succinctly recognizes that the intended surgery was not performed, to deny liability for four years and then force the plaintiff to incur costs of aborted discoveries suggests an intentional strategy of delay. I am troubled: this does not accord with the objectives described in the CMPA Strategic Plan. Plaintiffs don't have the war chest and endurance of professional defendants."

Frazer v. Haukioja (2008 CanLII 68149 [ON SC]; *canlii.ca/t/220f8*). The plaintiffs won their malpractice case, nevertheless, Justice Moore wrote, "Owing to the defendant's scorched earth policy of putting the plaintiffs to the test of establishing virtually all of their claims on all issues of damages and liability, the trial extended over some 20 days. Central issues were complex and vigorously contested."

In his judgment in *Ornstein v. Starr*, Master Short reproduced this transcript of the testimony of the CMPA witness with his own comments. Note that the term *discovery* is used to describe a procedure to obtain information before trial through demands for production of documents, depositions of parties and potential witnesses, written interrogatories (questions and answers written under oath), written requests for admissions of fact, examination of the scene, and the petitions and motions employed to enforce discovery rights. The theory of broad rights of discovery is that all parties will go to trial with as much knowledge as possible.

HEARD: June 29, 2011

REASONS FOR DECISION

Seven Words of Discovery

1. **Q.** Please state your full name for the record
   A. *Joseph Auby Starr.*

2. **Q.** And you are a doctor

   A. *I am.*

3. **Q.** And do you have a specialty?

   A. *Plastic surgery.*

4. **Q.** And how long have you been carrying on as a plastic surgeon?

   Counsel: Don't answer that.

I. Motion

[1] While the transcript of the above examination continues for eight pages, the witness, defendant doctor, is not recorded as uttering another word on his examination for discovery.

[2] The examination was held in January of 2011 with respect to a medical malpractice action, which arose out of an incident that occurred on July 13, 2006.

[3] Unfortunately, on that date the defendant surgeon mistakenly operated on the plaintiff's thumb instead of her right fifth finger in an operation performed at North York General Hospital.

[4] The defendant hospital in turn refused to even produce a witness for discovery in this case.

[69] It seems to me difficult to refer to the proposed questions as a "fishing expedition" when the boat seems to still be firmly tied up to the dock.

X. Disposition

[70] When all is said and done my goal is to promote a fair and just system. If patients are proven to have been harmed as a result of negligent medical care (or it is admitted that this is the case) fairness must dictate that timely arrangements be made to compensate those patients in an appropriate and timely manner. I cannot imagine that any defendant would attempt to rag the puck in an attempt to exhaust the injured party's finances or spirit. Certainly such an approach would not accord in any way with my view of fairness.

[71] Fairness and justice dictate the clear need for timely resolution of medico-legal matters. Regardless of the circumstances, medico-legal matters are stressful for all involved: physicians, other health care providers, patients and their families. I fail to see how the apparent tactics and strategy adopted in this case, "actively promote measures that respect the right to procedural fairness and encourage the timely resolution of such matters."

[72] It has not been demonstrated to me that this approach could possibly "improve accessibility to justice and reduce the stress experienced by physicians and their patients."

[73] After warning the defendant that the examination would be aborted and resort to a motion if the Doctor did not answer proper questions, his counsel continued to refuse to allow him to answer proper questions. The following exchange occurred between questions 14 and 19:

14. **Q.** In any event, Dr. Starr, when did you first meet the plaintiff, Sophie Ornstein?

Mr. Sutton: Don't answer that.

Anything relating to care has been admitted.

15. Mr. Linden: Well, I haven't asked about care yet. I am going to ask about his observations of the condition of her hand before he performed the surgery.

Mr. Sutton: Don't answer that.

16. Okay. Let's just go off the record.

17. Mr. Linden: I am going to ask three more if you object to all of them, we are just going to stop, just go to court, and we will have a court order your client to answer questions he is supposed to.

Mr. Sutton: No. You can put the questions on the record and establish the relevance....

18. Mr. Linden: No. I am going to ask three more questions.

Mr. Sutton: No. You can establish the relevance of your questions. If your question is relevant, I will allow him to answer. You haven't established the relevance of your question.

19. Mr. Linden: we are going to try three more and then we will call it a day.

Mr. Sutton: That is your choice.

20. **Q.** Sir, when did you first meet Sophie Ornstein?

Mr. Sutton: Don't answer that.

21. **Q.** Did you examine her hands at the time when you met her?

Mr. Sutton: Don't answer that

22. **Q.** Did you made any observations of the condition of her fingers when you first examined her?

Mr. Sutton: Don't answer that

Mr. Linden: Okay. That is enough.

[74] In my view it is indeed enough. Enough to justify making the order sought with costs on a substantial indemnity basis, payable forthwith.

When filing a medical malpractice lawsuit use a lawyer who will work on a contingency-fee basis and assume the risk of the $100,000+ estimated cost of the average trial. If you win, or get a settlement, the lawyer wins (about a third of the compensation.). If you lose, the lawyer should pay all fees and costs.

Another consideration is finding expert witnesses. *Don't sue without respectable, independent experts who will testify that a physician was negligent, and that negligence hurt the patient.* In civil liability cases, courts give much credence to evidence presented through expert testimony.

Make sure your Statement of Claim is unassailable. Claims for malpractice must be filed within a strict limitation period. Be prepared as well for a Motion to Strike the claim because it is allegedly unarguable in law, frivolous, or vexatious. This is usually only a delaying tactic that is meant to wear you down and force a settlement. Become familiar with the Supreme Court decision in *Hunt v. Carey Canada Inc. (1990) SCC 90.* It provides strict rules for when a Statement of Claim can, and cannot, be struck.

Finally, *understand that once a malpractice lawsuit is filed, the bills for witnesses, hearings, court fees, and lawyers on both sides start piling up.* If the costs become intolerable to the point of forcing you to drop the suit, all the costs to both parties could be yours to pay.

Ask yourself whether the damages to be claimed are worth the financial and physical toll they will take. You may win the case but lose your shirt. Or your life may be totally consumed by the ongoing litigation. Sure, your story may be interesting and your stand on principle against medical malpractice may be admirable, but at what cost?

Currently, medical malpractice lawsuits are a crapshoot where the rules and resources overwhelmingly favour defendants with deep pockets. There are several simple solutions, though, that can even the playing field and punish negligent or incompetent health workers without the plaintiffs risking their life's savings.

For decades, New Zealand and some Nordic countries have used a no-fault system with pre-set amounts paid to malpractice victims. Similar to the no-fault laws used in some Canadian provinces for car-accident victims, no-fault malpractice damages would be automatic, awarded quickly, and not diluted by legal costs. And, most importantly, although doctors and nurses wouldn't be legally blamed for mistakes, those health workers who generate the most complaints would be clearly identified through administrative courts. This is a critical shortcoming in medical treatment today, says the American Association for Justice in its February 2011 Report on Medical Negligence (*www.justice.org/resources/Medical_ Negligence_Primer.pdf*):

> Every profession has its bad apples and physicians are no exception. Just six percent of doctors are responsible for nearly 60 percent of all medical negligence, and the civil justice system is the only effective means for holding them accountable. Other disciplinary mechanisms are woefully inadequate. State medical boards, for instance, are supposed to discipline doctors who consistently violate standards of care. Yet two-thirds of doctors who make 10 or more medical negligence payments are never disciplined at all. Hospitals are on the front lines of patient safety, yet nearly half of all U.S. hospitals have never reported a disciplinary action to the National Practitioner Databank since its creation in 1990.

This is where a complaint moves beyond indemnity into the realm of social justice. By exposing the estimated six percent of doctors who elicit an estimated 60 percent of malpractice incidents we can correct the system that allows this to happen. This is what we did in the 1980s tainted-blood scandal in Canada, which produced much-needed reforms after extensive public hearings where guilt was assessed and reforms instituted.

Medical Treatments of Dubious Value

Consumers and physicians need to be wary of the overuse of medical tests and procedures that provide little benefit and in some cases may do harm.

Choosing Wisely is an initiative of the ABIM Foundation (*www. choosingwisely.org/doctor-patient-lists*). Its recommendations are meant to spur conversation about what is appropriate and necessary treatment. United States medical specialty societies representing more than 500,000 physicians have developed lists of things physicians and patients should question in recognition of the importance of physician and patient conversations to improve care and eliminate unnecessary tests and procedures.

These lists represent specific, evidence-based recommendations physicians and patients should discuss to help make wise decisions about the most appropriate care based on their individual situation. Each list provides information on when tests and procedures may be appropriate, as well as the methodology used in its creation.

I have summarized the recommendations of three of the twenty-six societies in Appendix C. I urge readers to go to the above-cited website for other recommendations.

VACATION NIGHTMARES

When we go on vacation we expect only good things will happen to us. However, the sheer number of providers of different services for the week or two you are in their hands, means some unpleasant experiences are bound to occur. The first issue to decide is whether or not an incident is worth an admonishment, an argument, or a formal request for compensation.

A lot depends upon how you and your family have been affected. Nevertheless, here are some specific deficiencies that automatically require some restitution from the sellers of your trip:

- injury, accidents, or close calls;

- unsafe conveyances and negligent handling of transportation;

- major items that are not as advertised, including quality of room and food, location of hotel, and overall security, cleanliness, and tranquility;

- extra charges or unavailability of items or services that were considered part of the trip costs;

- delays and missed excursions or transfers.

If any of the above occurs, immediately speak with the tour leader and email the travel provider. Take pictures of everything. If travelling in a group elect a spokesperson for that group.

Finally, as you continue making a "paper trail" of what is going wrong, *save the biggest battle for when you return home.* There, with the travel agent nearby, your request for compensation has a better chance of being granted since most of the possible intervenors who can help (travel agent, travel agent association, Canadian Transportation Agency, and small claims court) aren't far away.

Now two rules to remember when asking for compensation:

- There are guidelines everywhere, but they aren't immutable; *ask for what you feel is fair.*

- *Don't accept the sloughing off of responsibility.* Negligence flows upstream as well as downstream. The travel agent should have known better, the airline could have taken more precautions, and the tour operator, hotel, and excursion providers could have been more helpful. Under *Donoghue*, they all have a duty of care which they share.

Jarvis v. Swans Tours Ltd [1972] EWCA Civ 8 is an English contract law case on the measure of damages for disappointing breaches of contract. Here is Wikipedia's summary of Mr. Jarvis's "unforgettable vacation":

> Mr. Jarvis was a solicitor for Barking Council. He chose to go for Christmas holiday in Switzerland. He got a brochure from Swan Tours Ltd, which for Mörlialp, Giswil said the attractions were:
> "House Party Centre with special resident host ... Mörlialp is a most wonderful little resort on a sunny plateau ... Up there you will find yourself in the midst of beautiful alpine scenery, which in winter becomes a wonderland of sun, snow and ice, with a wide variety of fine ski-runs, a skating rink and exhilarating toboggan run ... Why did we choose the Hotel Krone ... mainly and most of all because of the 'Gemütlichkeit' and friendly welcome you will receive from Herr and Frau Weibel. ... The Hotel Krone has its own Alphütte Bar which will be open several evenings a week. ... No doubt you will be in for a great time, when you book this houseparty holiday ... Mr. Weibel, the charming owner, speaks English."
> In a special yellow box it said:
> "Swans House Party in Mörlialp. All these House Party arrangements are included in the price of your holiday. Welcome party on arrival. Afternoon tea and cake for 7 days. Swiss dinner by candlelight. Fondue party. Yodeler evening. Chali farewell party in the 'Alphütte Bar'. Service of representative."
> It also stated, "Hire of Skis, Sticks and Boots ... Ski Tuition ... 12 days £11.10." Mr. Jarvis booked 15 days with a ski pack

in August 1969 for £63.45, including Christmas supplement. He flew from Gatwick to Zurich on December 20, 1969, and returned on January 3, 1970. He found the "house party" was only 13 people in the first week and none in the second week. Mr. Weibel could not speak English. As Lord Denning [the judge who wrote the decision] said:

"So there was Mr. Jarvis, in the second week, in this hotel with no house party at all, and no one could speak English, except himself. He was very disappointed, too, with the skiing. It was some distance away at Giswil. There were no ordinary length skis. There were only mini-skis, about 3 ft. long. So he did not get his skiing as he wanted to. In the second week he did get some longer skis for a couple of days, but then, because of the boots, his feet got rubbed and he could not continue even with the long skis. So his skiing holiday, from his point of view, was pretty well ruined."

There were also no Swiss cakes, just crisps and little dry nut cakes. The "yodeler" was a local man who came in work clothes and sang four or five songs quickly. The "Alphütte Bar" was empty and only open one evening.

Mr. Jarvis sued for breach of contract. Lord Denning held that Mr. Jarvis could recover damages for the cost of his holiday, but also damages for "disappointment, the distress, the upset and frustration caused by the breach." Accordingly, Mr. Jarvis was awarded £125.

Car Rental Fraud

Have you checked your last car rental receipts? Dollar Rent A Car is facing a federal consumer fraud class-action lawsuit (*Sandra McKinnon v. Dollar Thrifty Automotive Group, Inc. d/b/a Dollar Rent a Car, et al.*, Case No. 12-cv-4457) that says the car rental company bilked customers out of millions of dollars by signing them up for insurance and other services they didn't want. The suit claims:

> Over the last four years Dollar has implemented a systematic program nationwide through which its employees and agents illegally dupe customers into signing up for collision damage waiver ("CDW"), car insurance and other added services that consumers have specifically declined. This is not an isolated incident with one consumer, but rather a systematic pattern of conduct that has occurred at a number of Dollar locations located throughout the United States.

Dollar has received multiple complaints about these issues but incentivizes its employees to make such sales, even by illegal means. If employees fail to obtain an average 30 per day upsales of additional options for three months they may be terminated and not eligible for unemployment. Employees are thus incentivized to take advantage of the customers' irritation, long lines, and misleading or high pressure sales tactics, by just telling them to tap certain lines to decline coverage when it may have the opposite result, or simply forge their signature.

Cruise Line Shortcomings

Cruise lines are responsible for the safety of everyone on board, and for ensuring that passengers enjoy the benefits of their trip as represented by travel brochures, travel agents, and the cruise line itself. When the trip is compromised by accidents, illness and disease, mechanical failures, missed destinations, deteriorating living conditions, and services of lesser quality than advertised, liability is shared by all of the tour promoters. This entails that crew members, especially, make sure illness and disease don't spread among those aboard a vessel. When an incident onboard or an accident does take place, whether it is a medical complication resulting from disease, an injury related to a slip and fall, or a passenger going overboard, the cruise line may share responsibility for any injuries or fatalities.

Furthermore, if investigations of the Carnival *Triumph* fire last February uncover that either the fire itself or the delay in docking contributed to any illnesses or injuries on board the vessel, this also can be considered a violation of passenger safety.

Carnival has offered *Triumph* passengers a "full refund of the cruise and transportation expenses, a future cruise credit equal to the amount paid for the voyage, reimbursement of all shipboard purchases made during the voyage, with the exception of casino, gift shop and artwork purchases, and further compensation of $500 per person."

This compensation package is quite common among cruise lines and is likely to be accepted by many passengers, who may not have much choice inasmuch as Carnival isn't a U.S. corporation and is not subject to U.S. taxes or other laws, a factor which prevents victims from making a full recovery following cruise ship accidents and injuries. An additional complication is deciding where to file a claim and finding lawyers willing to work for a contingency fee of about one-third of the approved settlement.

Hotels.com

A consumer fraud class-action against *Hotels.com* seeks restitution and class damages for breach of contract and unjust enrichment. The action says *Hotels.com* will not back up its promise: "After you book with *Hotels.com*, if you find a lower publicly available rate on line for the same dates, hotel, and room category, we will match the price and refund you the difference." Instead, the lawsuit states, "*Hotels.com* has an arbitrary and undisclosed policy to refund only a portion of the difference between its rate and other, lower rates. For example, in this case, *Hotels.com* stated that 'we can only refund you $142,'" even though the price difference was $215.

VEHICLES

Key Court Decisions

The following Canadian lawsuits and judgments cover typical problems that are likely to arise. *Use them as leverage when negotiating a settlement or as a reference should your claim go to trial.* Legal principles applying to Canadian and American law are similar; however, Quebec court decisions may be based on legal principles that don't apply outside that province. You can find a comprehensive listing of Canadian decisions from small claims courts all the way to the Supreme Court of Canada at *www.canlii.org* (Canadian Legal Information Institute).

CASE SUMMARY

Gibbons v. Trapp Motors Ltd. (1970; 9 D.L.R. [3rd], No. 742 [B.C.S.C.]): The court ordered the dealer to take back a new car that had numerous defects and required thirty-two hours of repairs. The refund was reduced by mileage driven.

Johnson v. Northway Chevrolet Oldsmobile (1993; 108 Sask. R., No. 138 [Q.B.]): The court ordered the dealer to take back a new car that had been brought in for repairs on fourteen different occasions. Two years after the car's purchase, the buyer initiated a lawsuit for the purchase price and general damages. General damages were awarded.

> *Julien v. GM of Canada* (1991; 116 N.B.R. [2nd], No. 80): The plaintiff's new diesel truck produced excessive engine noise. The dealer claimed that the problem was caused by the owner's engine alterations. The plaintiff was awarded the $5,000 cost of repairing the engine through an independent dealer.
>
> *Magna Management Ltd. v. Volkswagen Canada Inc.* (May 27, 1988; Vancouver [B.C.C.A.]; No. CA006037): This precedent-setting case allowed the plaintiff to keep his new $48,325 VW while awarding him $37,101 — three years after the car was purchased. The problems were centred on poor engine performance. The jury accepted the plaintiff's view that the car was practically worthless with its inherent defects.

Additional court judgments can be found in the legal reference section of your city's main public library or at a nearby university law library. Ask the librarian for help in choosing the legal phrases that best describe your claim.

LexisNexis (*global.lexisnexis.com/ca*) and FindLaw (*www.find law.com*) are two useful Internet sites for legal research. Their main drawback, though, is that you may need to subscribe or use a lawyer's subscription to access jurisprudence and other areas of the sites. However, there *is* a free online summary of class actions filed in Canada at *classactionsincanada.blogspot.com*.

Safety-Related Failures

Cases involving sudden acceleration, chronic stalling, and ABS and airbag failures are not that difficult to win in Canada under the doctrine of *res ipsa loquitur* ("the thing speaks for itself"), meaning, in negligence cases, that liability is shown by the failure itself. In a nutshell, the exact cause doesn't have to be pinpointed, and judges are free to award damages by weighing the "balance of probabilities" as to fault.

This advantage found in Canadian law was laid out succinctly in the July 1, 1998, issue of the *Journal of Small Business Management* in its comparison of product liability laws on both sides of the border ("Effects of Product Liability Laws on Small Business" at *www.all business.com/legal/laws-government-regulations/691847-1.html*):

> Although in theory the Canadian consumer must prove all of the elements of negligence (*Farro v. Nutone Electrical Ltd.*

1990; Ontario Law Reform Commission 1979; Thomas 1989), most Canadian courts allow injured consumers to use a procedural aid known as *res ipsa loquitur* to prove their cases (*Nicholson v. John Deere Ltd. 1986*; *McMorran v. Dom. Stores Ltd. 1977*). Under *res ipsa loquitur*, plaintiffs must only prove that they were injured in a way that would not ordinarily occur without the defendant's negligence. It is then the responsibility of the defendant to prove that he was not negligent. As proving the negative is extremely difficult, this Canadian reversal of the burden of proof usually results in an outcome functionally equivalent to strict product liability (*Phillips v. Ford Motor Co. of Canada Ltd. 1971*; Murray 1988). This concept is reinforced by the principle that a Canadian manufacturer does not have the right to manufacture an inherently dangerous product when a method exists to manufacture that product without risk of harm. To do so subjects the manufacturer to liability even if the safer method is more expensive (*Nicholson v. John Deere Ltd. 1986*).

In *Jarvis v. Ford* (United States Second Circuit Court of Appeal, February 7, 2002), a judgment was rendered in favour of a driver who was injured when her six-day-old Ford Aerostar minivan suddenly accelerated as it was started and put into gear. What makes this decision unique is that the jury had no specific proof of a defect. The Court of Appeal agreed with the jury award, and Justice Sonia Sotomayor — now a Supreme Court Justice — gave these reasons for the court's verdict (Restatement [Third] of Torts: Product Liability § 3 [1998]):

A product may be found to be defective without proof of the specific malfunction:
It may be inferred that the harm sustained by the plaintiff was caused by a product defect existing at the time of sale or distribution, without proof of a specific defect, when the incident that harmed the plaintiff:

(a) was of a kind that ordinarily occurs as a result of product defect; and

(b) was not, in the particular case, solely the result of causes other than product defect existing at the time of sale or distribution.

Comment *c* to this section notes:

> [There is] no requirement that plaintiff prove what aspect of the product was defective. The inference of defect may be drawn under this Section without proof of the specific defect. Furthermore, quite apart from the question of what type of defect was involved, the plaintiff need not explain specifically what constituent part of the product failed. For example, if an inference of defect can be appropriately drawn in connection with the catastrophic failure of an airplane, the plaintiff need not establish whether the failure is attributable to fuel-tank explosion or engine malfunction.

Incidents of sudden acceleration or chronic stalling are quite common. However, they are often very difficult to diagnose, and individual cases can be treated very differently by federal safety agencies. Nevertheless, getting corroborative proof may be far easier in the future, now that the U.S. Department of Transportation under the National Highway Traffic Safety Administration will require that automakers install "black box" accident data recorders in all vehicles and give out their access codes to accident investigators. In fact, a number of impaired drivers have already been sent to jail in Canada based on black-box-accessed data.

Sudden acceleration is considered to be a safety-related problem — stalling, only sometimes. Never mind that a vehicle's sudden loss of power on a busy highway puts everyone's lives at risk. The same problem exists with engine and transmission powertrain failures, which are only occasionally considered to be safety-related. ABS and airbag failures, however, are universally considered to be life-threatening defects. If your vehicle manifests any of these conditions, here's what you need to do:

- *Get independent witnesses to confirm that the problem exists.* Your primary tools include an independent mechanic's verification, passenger accounts, downloaded data from your vehicle's data recorder, and lots of Internet browsing using *www.lemonaidcars. com* and Google's search engine. Notify the dealer or manufacturer by fax, email, or registered letter that you consider the problem to be a factory-induced, safety-related defect. Make sure you address your correspondence to the manufacturer's product liability or legal affairs department. At the dealership's service bay, make sure that every work order clearly states the problem as well as the number of previous attempts to fix it. (You should end up with a few complaint letters and a handful of work orders confirming that this is an ongoing deficiency.) If the dealer won't give you a copy of the work order because the work is a warranty claim, ask for a copy of the order number "in case your estate wishes to file a claim, pursuant to an accident." (This wording will get the service manager's attention.) *Leaving a paper trail is crucial* for any claim you may have later on, because it shows your concern and persistence, and it clearly indicates that the dealer and manufacturer have had ample time to correct the defect.

- *Note on the work order that you expect the problem to be diagnosed and corrected under the emissions warranty or a "goodwill" program.* It also wouldn't hurt to add the phrase that "any deaths, injuries, or damage caused by the defect will be the dealer's and manufacturer's responsibility" because the work order (or letter, fax, or email) constitutes you putting them on "formal notice."

- *If the dealer does the necessary repairs at little or no cost to you, send a follow-up confirmation that you appreciate the "goodwill."* Also, emphasize that you'll be back if the problem reappears, even if the warranty has expired, because the repair renews your warranty rights applicable to that defect. In other words, the warranty clock is set back to its original position. Understand that you won't likely get a copy of the repair bill, either, because dealers don't like to admit that there was a serious defect present and don't feel that they owe you a copy of the work order if the repair was done *gratis.* You can, however, *subpoena the complete vehicle file from the dealer and manufacturer* (this costs about $50) if the case goes to small claims or a higher court. This request has produced many out-of-court settlements when the internal documents show extensive work was carried out to correct the problem.

- *If the problem persists, send a letter, fax, or email to the dealer and manufacturer saying so*, look for ALLDATA service bulletins to confirm that your vehicle's defects are factory-related, and report the failure by contacting Transport Canada (*www.tc.gc.ca/roadsafety/safevehicles/defectinvestigations/index.htm* or 1-800-333-0510) or the U.S. National Highway Traffic Safety Administration.

- The NHTSA's website (*www.safercar.gov*) will give you immediate access to five essential database categories applicable to your vehicle and model year: the latest recalls, current and closed safety investigations, defects reported by other owners, warranty extensions applied in other countries, and a brief summary of service bulletins listed by car model and year. The internal service bulletins are a "smoking gun" where the carmaker alerts the dealer as to which part is likely faulty, how much time is needed to fix the problem, and how much of a discount to give the customer. The written complaints often include tips as to easier fixes, as shown in the Ford Fusion incident reported below.

- Also, you may want to involve the non-profit, Montreal-based Automobile Protection Association or the Nader-founded Center for Auto Safety in Washington, D.C. (*www.autosafety.org/auto-defects*) to get a lawyer referral and an information sheet covering the problem.

- Now come two crucial questions: Repair the defect now or later? Use the dealer or an independent? Generally, it's smart to use an independent garage if you know the dealer isn't pushing for free corrective repairs from the manufacturer, if weeks or months have passed without any resolution of your claim, if the dealer keeps repeating that it's a maintenance item, and if you know an independent mechanic who will give you a detailed work order showing the defect is factory-related. Don't mention that a court case may ensue, since this will scare the dickens out of your only independent witness. An added bonus is that the repair charges will be about half of what a dealer would demand. Incidentally, if the automaker later denies warranty "goodwill" because you used an independent repairer, use the argument that the defect's safety implications required emergency repairs, carried out by whoever could see you first.

- Dashboard-mounted warning lights usually come on prior to airbags suddenly deploying, ABS brakes failing, or engine glitches causing the vehicle to stall out. (Sudden acceleration usually occurs without warning.) Automakers consider these lights to be critical safety warnings and generally advise drivers in the owner's manual to immediately have their vehicle serviced to correct the problem when they come on. This fact bolsters the argument that your life was threatened, emergency repairs were required, and your request for another vehicle or a complete refund isn't out of line.

- Sudden acceleration can have multiple causes, isn't easy to duplicate, and is often blamed on the driver mistaking the accelerator for the brakes or failing to perform proper maintenance. Yet NHTSA data show that with the 1992–2000 Explorer, for example, a faulty cruise-control or PCV valve and poorly mounted pedals are the most likely causes of the Explorer's sudden acceleration. To satisfy the burden of proof that the problem exists and is the automaker's responsibility, use the legal doctrine called "the balance of probabilities" by eliminating all of the possible dodges the dealer or manufacturer may employ. Show that proper maintenance has been carried out, you're a safe driver, and the incident occurs frequently and without warning.

- *If any of the above defects causes an accident, or if the airbag fails to deploy or you're injured by its deployment, ask your insurance company to have the vehicle towed to a neutral location and clearly state that neither the dealer nor the automaker should touch the vehicle until your insurance company and Transport Canada have completed their investigation.* Also, get as many witnesses as possible and immediately go to the hospital for a check-up, even if you're feeling okay. You may be injured and not know it because the adrenalin coursing through your veins is masking your injuries. A hospital exam will easily confirm that your injuries are accident-related, which is essential evidence for court or for future settlement negotiations.

- *Peruse NHTSA's online accident and service bulletin database* to find reports of other accidents caused by the same failure, bulletins that indicate part upgrades, current defect investigations, and reported failures that have resulted in recalls or closed investigations.

- *Don't let your insurance company bully you.* Refuse to let them settle the case if you're sure the accident was caused by a mechanical failure. Even if an engineering analysis fails to directly implicate the manufacturer or dealer, you can always plead the aforementioned balance of probabilities. If the insurance company settles, your insurance premiums will soar and the manufacturer will get away with the perfect crime.

Warranty Runaround

Sometimes dealers will do all sorts of minor repairs that don't correct the problem, and then, after the warranty runs out, they'll tell you that major repairs are needed. You can prevent this nasty surprise by repeatedly bringing your vehicle into the dealership before the warranty ends. During each visit, insist that a written work order include the specific nature of the problem as *you* see it and that the work order carry the notation that this is the second, third, or fourth time the same problem has been brought to the dealer's attention. Write it down yourself, if need be. This allows you to show a pattern of nonperformance by the dealer during the warranty period and establishes that it's a serious and chronic problem. When the warranty expires, you have the legal right to demand that it be extended on those items consistently reappearing on your handful of work orders. *Lowe v. Fairview Chrysler* is an excellent judgment that reinforces this important principle. In another lawsuit, *François Chong v. Marine Drive Imported Cars Ltd. and Honda Canada Inc.*, a Honda owner forced Honda to fix his engine six times — until they got it right.

A retired GM service manager gave me another effective tactic to use when you're not sure that a dealer's warranty "repairs" will actually correct the problem for a reasonable period of time after the warranty expires:

> When you pick up the vehicle after the warranty repair has been done, hand the service manager a note to be put in your file that says you appreciate the warranty repair; however, you intend to return and ask for further warranty coverage if the problem reappears before a reasonable amount of time has elapsed even if the original warranty has expired. A copy of the same note should be sent to the automaker.... Keep your copy of the note in the glove compartment as cheap insurance against paying for a repair that wasn't fixed correctly the first time.

Safety restraints, such as airbags and seat belts, have warranty coverage extended for the lifetime of the vehicle, following an agreement made between U.S. automakers and importers. In Canada, though, some automakers try to dodge this responsibility because they are incorporated as separate Canadian companies. That distinction didn't fly with B.C.'s Court of Appeal in the 2002 *Robson* decision (*www.courts.gov.bc.ca/jdb-txt/ca/02/03/2002bcca0354.htm*).

In that class-action petition, the court declared that both Canadian companies *and* their American counterparts can be held liable in Canada for deceptive acts that violate the provincial *Trade Practices Act.*

How fairly a warranty is applied is more important than how long it remains in effect. Once you know the normal wear rate for a mechanical component or body part, *you can demand proportional compensation when you get less than normal durability* — no matter what the original warranty said.

Aftermarket products and services — such as gas-saving gadgets, rustproofing, and paint protectors — can render the manufacturer's warranty invalid, so *make sure you're in the clear before purchasing any optional equipment or services from an independent supplier.*

Some dealers tell customers that they need to have original-equipment parts installed in order to maintain their warranty. A variation on this theme requires that routine servicing — including tune-ups and oil changes (with a certain brand of oil) — be done by the selling dealer, or the warranty is invalidated.

Nothing could be further from the truth. Canadian law stipulates that whoever issues a warranty cannot make that warranty conditional on the use of any specific brand of motor oil, oil filter, or any other component, unless it's provided to the customer free of charge.

False Advertising and Fuel-Economy Misrepresentation

When you're buying a new vehicle, the seller can't misrepresent the vehicle through a lie or a failure to disclose important information. Typical scenarios are odometer turnbacks, accident damage, used or leased cars sold as new, new vehicles that are the wrong colour or the wrong model year, or vehicles that lack promised options or standard features.

CASE SUMMARY

Goldie v. Golden Ears Motors (1980) Ltd. (Port Coquitlam; June 27, 2000; British Columbia Small Claims Court; Case No. CO8287; Justice Warren): In a well-written eight-page judgment, the court awarded plaintiff Goldie $5,000 for engine repairs on a 1990 Ford F-150 pickup in addition to $236 court costs. The dealer was found to have misrepresented the mileage and sold a used vehicle that didn't meet Section 8.01 of the provincial motor vehicle regulations (unsafe tires, defective exhaust and headlights).

> In rejecting the seller's defence that he disclosed all information "to the best of his knowledge and belief," as stipulated in the sales contract, Justice Warren stated the following:
>
> > The words "to the best of your knowledge and belief" do not allow someone to be willfully blind to defects or to provide incorrect information. I find as a fact that the business made no effort to fulfill its duty to comply with the requirements of this form. The defendant has been reckless in its actions. More likely, it has actively deceived the claimant into entering into this contract. I find the conduct of the defendant has been reprehensible throughout the dealings with the claimant.
>
> This judgment closes a loophole that sellers have used to justify their misrepresentation, and it allows for the cancellation of the sale and damages if the vehicle doesn't meet highway safety regulations.

A California class action lawsuit over the fuel economy claims for the 2013 Ford C-Max and Fusion Hybrid accuses Ford of making "false and misleading" claims and cites tests by *Consumer Reports* that found both hybrids burned much more fuel than their EPA claims. It is the third automaker this year found to be making untrue gas mileage claims. Honda and Hyundai have set up $200 refund programs to compensate their owners; Ford will likely do the same.

In *Paduano v. American Honda Motor Co., Inc.*, Honda paid $50,000 plus another $50,000 in attorneys' fees for misleading fuel claims with its Civic Hybrid model. Interestingly, Honda America is now offering only $200 refunds to owners of 2003–09 Civic Hybrids and extending the cars' warranty in a class-action settlement in the United States (see *https://hchsettlement.com/Notice.aspx*). Canadians aren't part of the settlement, but a small claims court judge can award the same amount or more in Canada on a case-by-case basis.

Coincidentally, a few months ago Hyundai and Kia lowered the fuel economy ratings for all of their 2011–13 model-year vehicles and announced a fuel refund program for affected owners. Overall, they had overstated fuel economy ratings for about 900,000 vehicles, or 35 percent of the 2011–13 model year vehicles.

Canadian provincial courts are also cracking down on deceptive sales practices, and the misrepresentation of fuel economy figures is squarely in the judiciary's sights. Ontario's *Consumer Protection Act, 2002* (*www.e-laws.gov.on.ca/html/statutes/english/elaws_statutes_02c30_e.htm*), for example, lets a vehicle buyer cancel a contract within one year of entering into an agreement if their dealer made a false, misleading, deceptive, or unconscionable representation. This law means that new- or used-car dealers cannot make the excuse that they were fooled about the condition or performance of a vehicle, or that they were simply providing data supplied by the manufacturer. The law clearly states that both parties are jointly liable and that dealers are *presumed* to know the history, quality, and true performance of what they are selling.

Important details like fuel economy *can* lead to a contract's cancellation if the dealer gives a higher-than-actual figure. In *Sidney v. 1011067 Ontario Inc. (c.o.b. Southside Motors)*, a precedent-setting case that was filed before Ontario's *Consumer Protection Act* was toughened in 2002, the buyer was awarded $11,424.51 plus prejudgment interest because of a false representation made by the defendant regarding fuel efficiency. The plaintiff claimed that the defendant advised him that the vehicle had a range of 800–900 kilometres per tank of fuel when, in fact, the maximum distance was only 500 kilometres per tank.

These consumer victories are particularly important as fuel prices soar and everyone from automakers to sellers of ineffective gas-saving gadgets make outlandishly false fuel economy claims. Not surprisingly, sellers try to use the expressed warranty to reject claims, while *smart plaintiffs ignore the written warranty and argue for a refund under the implied warranty, judgments, and settlements.*

Automobile Infotainment Devices

During the past decade, infotainment interfaces have transformed automobiles into mobile computer systems that are easy prey to heat, cold, moisture, and vibration. "It would be easy to say the modern car is a computer on wheels, but it's more like thirty or more computers on wheels," said Bruce Emaus, the chairman of SAE International's embedded software standards committee. Even basic vehicles have at least thirty of these microprocessor-controlled devices, known as electronic control units, and some luxury cars have as many as a hundred.

And yet these systems — which govern the car's navigation, hands-free calling connectivity, music and media management, and wrap it all together with a single go-to interface — can be distracting, non-responsive, failure-prone, and expensive to troubleshoot and fix.

Whichever system is chosen — MyFord Touch (Ford), CUE (Cadillac/GM), iDrive (BMW), COMAND (Mercedes-Benz), MMI (Audi), and Uconnect Touch (Chrysler) — they all have many things that can and do go wrong: a display screen; a rotary or toggle controller; voice control; and some back-up buttons on the dash and/or steering wheel.

There is growing discontent with the hands-free features and original-equipment navigation systems and interfaces found in today's automobiles. Hands-free systems often failed to recognize voice commands and other owner-reported problems increased by 137 percent in four years.

Smartphones are filling the gap, says the market research firm J.D. Power and Associates' 2012 U.S. Navigation Usage and Research Study: 47 percent of vehicle owners say they use a smartphone application for navigation in the vehicle, while 46 percent said that they either "definitely would not" or "probably would not" purchase another factory-installed navigation system.

Two class-action claims are working their way through the courts in the United States:

CASE SUMMARY

Richards v. Ford Motor Co. (February 28, 2012; Case No. 2:12-cv-00543): Some of the problems include blank screens, missing presets, lack of voice recognition, incorrect dialing of phone numbers, and display problems with the backup camera. The plaintiff argues that the defects have diminished the value of the vehicles.

Steven Rouse, et al. v. Ford Motor Company (Case No. 11-CH-20581, Circuit Court of Cook County, Illinois, County Department, Chancery Division): This class-action lawsuit seeks actual damages, punitive damages, and other relief under the *Illinois Consumer Fraud Act*, including breach of warranty, common law fraud, and unjust enrichment. Ford sold vehicles with a factory-installed GPS navigation system called SYNC that does not contain all the advertised features. As a result, the class action lawsuit alleges, consumers bought vehicles and paid for upgraded navigation systems based on erroneous advertisements. Missing are the Traffic, Directions, and Information (TDI) feature and voice activation.

Paint and Body Defects

The following settlement advice applies mainly to paint defects, but you can use these tips for any other vehicle defect that you believe is the automaker's or dealer's responsibility.

Four good examples of favourable paint judgments are *Shields v. General Motors of Canada*; *Bentley v. Dave Wheaton Pontiac Buick GMC Ltd. and General Motors of Canada*; *Maureen Frank v. General Motors of Canada Limited*; and the most recent, *Dunlop v. Ford of Canada*.

In your claim letter, one of the best judgments to cite is the *Frank* decision (No. SC#12 [2001]; Saskatchewan Provincial Court, Saskatoon, Saskatchewan; October 17, 2001; Provincial Court Judge H.G. Dirauf):

> On June 23, 1997, the Plaintiff bought a 1996 Chevrolet Corsica from a General Motors dealership. At the time, the odometer showed 33,172 km. The vehicle still had some factory warranty. The car had been a lease car and had no previous accidents.
>
> During June of 2000, the Plaintiff noticed that some of the paint was peeling off from the car and she took it to a General Motors dealership in Saskatoon and to the General Motors dealership in North Battleford where she purchased the car. While there were some discussions with the GM dealership about the peeling paint, nothing came of it and the Plaintiff now brings this action claiming the cost of a new paint job.
>
> During 1999, the Plaintiff was involved in a minor collision causing damage to the left rear door. This damage was repaired. During this repair some scratches to the left front door previously done by vandals were also repaired.
>
> The Plaintiff's witness, Frank Nemeth, is a qualified auto body repairman with some 26 years of experience. He testified that the peeling paint was a factory defect and that it was necessary to completely strip the car and repaint it. He diagnosed the cause of the peeling paint as a separation of the primer surface or colour coat from the electrocoat primer. In his opinion no primer surfacer was applied at all. He testified that once the peeling starts, it will continue. He has seen this problem on General Motors vehicles. The defect is called delamination.
>
> Mr. Nemeth stated that a paint job should last at least 10 years. In my opinion, most people in Saskatchewan grow up with cars and are familiar with cars. I think it is common knowledge that the original paint on cars normally lasts in excess of 15 years and that rust becomes a problem before the paint fails. In any event, paint peeling off, as it did on the Plaintiff's vehicle, is not common. I find that the paint on a new car put on by the factory should last at least 15 years.

> It is clear from the evidence of Frank Nemeth (independent body shop manager) that the delamination is a factory defect. His evidence was not seriously challenged. I find that the factory paint should not suffer a delamination defect for at least 15 years and that this factory defect breached the warranty that the paint was of acceptable quality and was durable for a reasonable period of time.
>
> There will be judgment for the Plaintiff in the amount of $3,412.38 plus costs of $81.29.

Some of the important aspects of the *Frank* judgment are:

- The judge accepted that the automaker was responsible, even though the car had been bought used. The subsequent purchaser wasn't prevented from making the warranty claim, even though the warranty had long since expired, both in time and mileage, and she was the second owner.

- The judge stressed that the provincial warranty can kick in when the automaker's warranty has expired or isn't applied.

- By awarding full compensation to the plaintiff, the judge didn't feel that there was a significant "betterment" or improvement added to the car that would warrant reducing the amount of the award.

- The judge decided that the paint delamination was a factory defect, and that without this factory defect a paint job should last up to fifteen years.

- GM offered to pay $700 of the paint repairs if the plaintiff dropped the suit; the judge awarded five times that amount.

- Maureen Frank won this case despite having to confront GM lawyer Ken Ready, who had considerable experience arguing other paint cases for GM and Chrysler.

Automobile Tires

Consumers have gained additional rights following Bridgestone/Firestone's massive tire recall in 2001. Because of the confusion and chaos surrounding Firestone's handling of the recall, Ford's dealers stepped into the breach and replaced the tires with any equivalent tires dealers had in stock, no questions asked.

This is an important precedent that tears down the traditional liability wall separating tire manufacturers from automakers in product liability claims. In essence, whoever sells the product can now be held liable for damages. Canadian consumers now have an easier time holding the dealer, auto-maker, and tire-maker liable, not just for recalled products but also for any defect that affects the safety or reasonable durability of that product. This includes tire valve stem failures as well as tire pressure monitoring systems (TPMS).

CASE SUMMARY

Winnipeg Condominium v. Bird Construction ([1995] 1S.C.R.85): In this case, the Supreme Court of Canada ruled that defendants are liable in negligence for any designs that resulted in a risk to the public for safety or health. The Supreme Court reversed a long-standing policy and provided the public with a new cause of action that had not existed before in Canada. Prior to this Supreme Court ruling, companies dodged liability for falling bridges and crashing planes by warranty exclusion and "entire-agreement" contract clauses. In the *Winnipeg Condominium* case, the Supreme Court held that repairs made to prevent serious damage or accidents could be claimed from the designer or builder for the cost of repair in tort from any subsequent purchaser. Consumers with tire or other claims relating to the safety of their vehicles would be wise to insert the above court decision (with explanation) in their claim letter and then mail or fax it to the automaker's legal affairs or product liability department. A copy should also be deposited with the clerk of the small claims court, if you have to use that recourse.

Blackwood v. Ford Motor Company of Canada Ltd. (2006; Provincial Court of Alberta, Civil Division; Docket: PO690101722; Registry: Canmore; 2006/12/08; Honourable J. Shriar): This four-page judgment gives important guidelines as to how a plaintiff can successfully claim a refund for a defective tire. The plaintiff bought a new 2005 Ford Focus. After ten months and 22,000 kilometres, his dealer said all four tires needed replacing at a cost of $560.68. Both the dealer and Ford refused to cover the expense under the three-year/60,000-kilometre manufacturer's tire warranty, alleging that the wear was "normal wear and tear." Judge Shriar disagreed and awarded the plaintiff the full cost of the replacement tires, plus the filing fee and costs related to the registered mail and corporate records address check. An additional $100 was awarded for court costs, plus interest on the total amount from the date of the filing.

CONCLUSION

Change means movement. Movement means friction. Only in the frictionless vacuum of a nonexistent abstract world can movement or change occur without that abrasive friction of conflict.

— Saul Alinsky, *Rules for Radicals*

You now have all the tools needed to participate fully as a consumer — ready to exercise your legal rights to obtain the quality of services and products you deserve from the wide range of companies that operate so freely within our economy. You have the means to judge when to complain and the know-how to do so forcefully, creatively, and effectively. The one thing that may still be missing for most of us Canadians is *attitude*. Although not normally featured in our national culture, attitude definitely helps when it comes to the art of complaining — and I think that armed with the information contained in this book, the necessary attitude for becoming an accomplished complainer can be cultivated.

I believe that through the dissemination of public-interest information, the mobilization of people at the grassroots level, the litigation of public issues, and the legislation of fundamental rights, Canadians forge their complaints into tools of social reform. The Rusty Ford Owners Association did it. The Raging Grannies and Greenpeace are doing it. And our nation's poor and homeless will always do it.

They know citizen power works. Especially when it's abrasive — when it gets up in your face and inspires respect through example and sustained, focused action. Citizens and citizen groups can bring a corporation to *fear* losing profits; make a politician *fear* withdrawal of support; threaten a professional to *fear* public censure; and teach business and government to *fear* the courts.

The French writer François Mauriac says that "fear is the beginning of wisdom" (*"La peur est le commencement de la sagesse"*). If that is truly so, then unleash that fear-inspired wisdom to create the justice we all seek.

SAMPLE LETTERS

Product Complaint Letter/Email/Fax

Without Prejudice

Date

Seller, Manufacturer, or Distributor Name and Address

Dear Sir or Madam,

Please be advised that I am dissatisfied with my _____ that I bought from you for the following reasons:

1. _____.
2. _____.
3. _____.

In compliance with Canadian consumer protection laws and the 'implied warranty" upheld by the Supreme Court of Canada in *Donoghue v. Stevenson and Kravitz v. GM*, I hereby request that these defects be repaired in the near future without charge, or the _____ taken back and my money refunded.

This product has not been reasonably durable, is not of merchantable quality, and is, therefore, not as represented to me.

Should you fail to repair these defects in a satisfactory manner and within a reasonable period of time, I reserve the right to have the repairs done elsewhere and claim reimbursement in court without further delay.

I also reserve my rights to punitive damages up to $1 million, pursuant to the Canadian Supreme Court's ruling in *Whiten v. Pilot* (February 22, 2002).

I believe your company wants to deal with its clients in an honest, competent manner and trust that my claim is the exception and not the rule.

A positive response within the next five (5) days would be appreciated.

Sincerely,

(signed with telephone number, email address, or fax number)

Product Complaint Letter/Email/Fax (Quebec Only)

Without Prejudice

Date

Seller, Manufacturer, or Distributor Name and Address

Dear Sir or Madam,

Please be advised that I am dissatisfied with my _____
that I bought from you for the following reasons:

1. _____ .
2. _____ .
3. _____ .

I am hereby invoking Quebec's *Civil Code Article 1726,* which states:

"The seller is bound to warrant the buyer that the property and its accessories are, at the time of the sale, free of latent defects which render it unfit for the use for which it was intended or which so diminish its usefulness that the buyer would not have bought it or paid so high a price if he had been aware of them."

I request that these defects be repaired in the near future without charge, or the _____ taken back and my money refunded.

This product has not been reasonably durable, is not of merchantable quality, and is, therefore, not as represented to me.

Should you fail to repair these defects in a satisfactory manner and within a reasonable period of time, I reserve the right to have the repairs done elsewhere and claim reimbursement in court without further delay.

I also reserve my rights to punitive damages up to $1 million, pursuant to the Canadian Supreme Court's ruling in *Whiten v. Pilot* (February 22, 2002).

I believe your company wants to deal with its clients in an honest, competent manner and trust that my claim is the exception and not the rule.

A positive response within the next five (5) days would be appreciated.

Sincerely,

(signed with telephone number, email address, or fax number)

Service Complaint Letter/Email/Fax

Without Prejudice

Date

Seller or Service Provider Name and Address

Dear Sir or Madam,

Please be advised that I am dissatisfied with the following service you pro-vided, namely _____, for these reasons:

1. _____.

2. _____.

3. _____.

You have not fulfilled our contract for services as specified. This is a clear vio-lation of Canadian consumer protection laws as upheld by both common and civil law statutes. I hereby request that you correct the deficiencies without delay and respect the terms of our contract. Failing which, I want my money refunded.

If my request is denied, I reserve the right under *Sharman v. Ford*, Ontario Superior Court of Justice, No. 17419/02SR, 2003/10/07, to have the contracted work done elsewhere. I shall then claim reimbursement in court for that cost, plus punitive damages for my stress and inconvenience, without further delay, pursuant to the Canadian Supreme Court's ruling in *Whiten v. Pilot*.

I am sure you want to deal with your clients in an honest, competent manner and trust that my claim is the exception and not the rule.

A positive response within the next five (5) days would be appreciated.

Sincerely,

(signed with telephone number, email address, or fax number)

Service Complaint Letter/Email/Fax (Quebec Only)

Without Prejudice

Date

Seller or Service Provider Name and Address

Dear Sir or Madam,

Please be advised that I am dissatisfied with the following service you sold to me, namely _____, for these reasons:

1. _____.
2. _____.
3. _____.

In compliance with Quebec's *Civil Code and Consumer Protection Act* provisions that contracts are to be respected, I hereby request that these services be corrected without delay in the near future and without charge. If that cannot be done, I want my money refunded.

Should you fail to provide these services in a satisfactory manner and within a reasonable period of time, I reserve the right to have the work done elsewhere and shall claim reimbursement in court without further delay.

If there are further delays, I also reserve my rights to punitive damages up to $1 million, pursuant to the Canadian Supreme Court's ruling in *Whiten v. Pilot* (February 22, 2002).

I believe your company wants to deal with its clients in an honest, competent manner and trust that my claim is the exception and not the rule.

A positive response within the next five (5) days would be appreciated.

Sincerely,

(signed with telephone number, email address, or fax number)

Electronic Device

Without Prejudice

Date

Seller, Manufacturer, or Distributor Name and Address

Dear Sir or Madam,

Please be advised that I am dissatisfied with my _____
that I bought from you. This is what is wrong:

1. _____.
2. _____.
3. _____.

In compliance with Canadian consumer protection laws and the "implied warranty" upheld by the Supreme Court of Canada in *Donoghue v. Stevenson, Kravitz v. GM*, and Apple's "Stipulation of Settlement", *In re Apple iPhone/iPod Warranty Litigation*; Case No. CV-10-1610, April 10, 2013, I hereby request that the [phone/electronic device] be replaced as soon as possible at no cost to me.

This product has not been reasonably durable, is not of merchantable quality, and is, therefore, not as represented to me.

Should you fail to replace this [phone/electronic device] in a satisfactory manner and within a reasonable period of time, I reserve the right to have the repairs or replacement done elsewhere by an independent retailer and claim reimbursement in court without further delay.

I also reserve my rights to punitive damages up to $1 million, pursuant to the Canadian Supreme Court's ruling in *Whiten v. Pilot* (February 22, 2002).

I believe your company wants to deal with its clients in an honest, competent manner and trust that my claim is the exception and not the rule.

A positive response within the next five (5) days would be appreciated.

Sincerely,

(signed with telephone number, email address, or fax number)

Contaminated Food

Without Prejudice

Date

Seller, Manufacturer, or Distributor Name and Address

Dear Sir or Madam,

Please be advised that I am dissatisfied with my purchase of _____
_____ that I bought from you on _____. Here are
the reasons:

1. _____.
2. _____.
3. _____.

No one expects to find toxic substances or foreign objects in the food they are
served or purchase off the shelf. Both the seller and provider of the contaminated food are responsible for the damages caused by their negligence.

Following the "implied warranty" and "negligence" doctrines upheld by
the Supreme Court of Canada in *Donoghue v. Stevenson,* where a snail was
found in a bottle of ginger beer *and Kravitz v. GM,* where both the seller and
manufacturer were held jointly responsible, I respectfully ask for reasonable
compensation for my mental distress and inconvenience, which I assess to be
$_____.

I also reserve my rights to punitive damages pursuant to the Canadian
Supreme Court's $1 million ruling in *Whiten v. Pilot.*

I certainly hope we can put this problem behind us. A positive response
within the next five (5) days would be appreciated.

Sincerely,

(signed with telephone number, email address, or fax number)

Vacation Nightmares

Without Prejudice

Date

Seller, Manufacturer, or Distributor Name and Address

Dear Sir or Madam,

Please be advised that I am dissatisfied with my purchase of _____
_____ that I bought from you on _____. Here are the
reasons and supporting documents:

1. _____.

2. _____.

3. _____.

As you can see from the above-mentioned deficiencies, this vacation was not as
represented, both from a quality and a personal safety perspective. We did not
have the pleasant experience we were counting upon. Both the seller and provider
of this travel product are responsible for the damages caused by their negligence.

Following the "implied warranty" and "negligence" doctrines upheld by
the Supreme Court of Canada in *Donoghue v. Stevenson and Kravitz v. GM*, the
sellers were held responsible for not delivering what was represented. I also
refer to *Jarvis v. Swan Tours*, as support of my contention that there was a
"breach of contract" justifying compensation for my "mental distress."

I cite Lord Denning, the presiding judge in *Swan*, who held that Mr. Jarvis
could recover damages for the cost of his holiday, but also damages for "disappointment, the distress, the upset and frustration caused by the breach."

I respectfully ask for your intervention and reasonable compensation for
this breach of contract, mental distress and inconvenience.

Should you fail to deal with this claim in a satisfactory manner and within
a reasonable period of time, I reserve the right to file an action in small-claims
court without further delay.

I also reserve my rights to punitive damages pursuant to the Canadian
Supreme Court's $1 million ruling in *Whiten v. Pilot*.

I certainly hope we can put this problem behind us. A positive response
within the next five (5) days would be appreciated.

Sincerely,

(signed with telephone number, email address, or fax number)

Fuel-Economy Misrepresentation

Without Prejudice

Date

Seller, Manufacturer, or Distributor Name and Address

Dear Sir or Madam,

Please be advised that I am dissatisfied with my _____ poor fuel economy. I bought this vehicle from you based upon your advertising that it would be fuel-efficient. It isn't. You indicated I could expect 12.7/8.3 L/100 km city/highway mileage but I am burning 14.7/10.3 L/100 km in careful, flat-highway driving.

I, therefore, seek $500 in compensation in compliance with *Sidney v. 1011067 Ontario Inc. (c.o.b. Southside Motors)* and provincial and federal misleading advertising statutes, upheld by the Supreme Court of Canada's recent award of punitive damages ($15,000) in *R. v. Time Inc.,* and ($10 million) in *R. v. Bell Canada.*

I also base my claim on the "implied warranty" of merchantability, and joint responsibility of automaker and dealer, also confirmed by the Supreme Court of Canada in *Donoghue v. Stevenson and Kravitz v. GM.*

This product is not as represented to me. Honda, in *Lockabey v. American Honda Motors*, Hyundai, and Kia have recently set up $200 owner refund programs and warranty extensions that compensate their customers misled by misrepresented fuel economy figures and faced with higher fuel costs. In *Paduano v. American Honda Motor Co., Inc.*, Honda later settled for $50,000, plus another $50,000 in attorneys' fees.

I also reserve my rights to punitive damages up to $1 million, pursuant to the Canadian Supreme Court's ruling in *Whiten v. Pilot* where an insurance settlement was unduly delayed.

I believe your company wants to settle these fuel-economy claims and move on. A positive response within the next five (5) days would be appreciated.

Sincerely,

(signed with telephone number, email address, or fax number)

Infotainment Device Failure

Without Prejudice

Date

Seller, Manufacturer, or Distributor Name and Address

Dear Sir or Madam,

Please be advised that I am dissatisfied with my car's Infotainment system
_____ that I bought from you. This is what is wrong:

1. _____.
2. _____.
3. _____.

I want these defects repaired or my vehicle replaced and my money refunded under the "implied warranty" doctrine upheld by the Supreme Court of Canada in *Donoghue v. Stevenson, Kravitz v. GM*, and Winnipeg Condominium v. Bird Construction *[1995] 1S.C.R.85* (negligence). I also cite two pending class-actions: *Richards v. Ford Motor Co., Case No. 2:12-cv-00543 and Steven Rouse, et al. v. Ford Motor Company*, Case No. 11-CH-20581, Circuit Court of Cook County, Illinois, County Department, Chancery Division.

This product has not been reasonably durable, is not of merchantable quality, and is, therefore, not as represented to me.

Should you fail to satisfy my claim in a satisfactory manner and within a reasonable period of time, I reserve the right to have the repairs done elsewhere by an independent garage and claim reimbursement in court without further delay.

I also reserve my rights to punitive damages up to $1 million, pursuant to the Canadian Supreme Court's ruling in *Whiten v. Pilot* (February 22, 2002).

I believe your company wants to deal with its clients in an honest, competent manner and trust that my claim is the exception and not the rule.

A positive response within the next five (5) days would be appreciated.

Sincerely,

(signed with telephone number, email address, or fax number)

Tire Defects or Premature Wear

Without Prejudice

Date

Seller, Manufacturer, or Distributor Name and Address

Dear Sir or Madam,

Please be advised that I am dissatisfied with my _____
that I bought from you for the following reasons:

1. _____.
2. _____.
3. _____.

In compliance with Canadian consumer protection laws and the "implied warranty" upheld by the Supreme Court of Canada in *Donoghue v. Stevenson, Kravitz v. GM*, Winnipeg Condominium v. Bird Construction *[1995] 1S.C.R.85* (negligence), and *Blackwood v. Ford Motor Company of Canada Ltd., 2006* (Provincial Court of Alberta, Civil Division; Docket: PO690101722; Registry: Canmore; 2006/12/08, I hereby request that the defective tire be replaced at no cost to me.

This product has not been reasonably durable, is not of merchantable quality, and is, therefore, not as represented to me.

Should you fail to deal with this claim in a satisfactory manner and within a reasonable period of time, I reserve the right to purchase a replacement from an independent retailer and claim reimbursement in court without further delay.

I also reserve my rights to punitive damages, pursuant to the Canadian Supreme Court's ruling in *Whiten v. Pilot* (February 22, 2002).

A positive response within the next five (5) days would be appreciated.

Sincerely,

(signed with telephone number, email address, or fax number)

Appendix B

REASONABLE DURABILITY

ACCESSORIES

Air conditioner	7 years	Power seats, locks	5 years
Cruise control	7 years/140,000 km	Radiator	5 years/100,000 km
Headlights (HID)	5 years/100,000 km	Radio	7 years
Hybrid battery	10 years	Tire pressure sensor	5 years
Power doors, windows	5 years		

BODY

Door handles	10 years/160,000 km	Rust (perforations)	7–11 years
Liftgate struts	7 years	Rust (surface)	5 years
Paint (peeling)	7–11 years	Water/wind/air leaks	5 years

BRAKE SYSTEM

ABS	100,000 km	Brake rotor	60,000 km
ABS computer	10 years/200,000 km	Brake calipers/pads	30,000 km
Brake drum	120,000 km	Master cylinder	100,000 km
Brake drum linings	35,000 km	Wheel cylinder	80,000 km

ENGINE AND DRIVETRAIN

CV joint	6 years/120,000 km	Oxygen sensor	10 years/200,000 miles
Differential	7 years/140,000 km	Powertrain (engine/	
Engine (diesel)	15 years/300,000 km	transmission)	10 years/200,000 miles
Engine (gas)	7 years/140,000 km	Transfer case	10 years/200,000 km
Engine block	7 years/no mileage	Transmission (auto.)	10 years/200,000 km
Engine control module	15 years/300,000 km	Transmission (man.)	12 years/240,000 km
Engine turbocharger	7 years/140,000 km	Transmission oil cooler	10 years/200,000 km
Fuel pump module	10 years/200,000 km		

EXHAUST SYSTEM

Catalytic converter	10 years/200,000 km	Muffler	3 years/60,000 km
Exhaust manifold	10 years/200,000 km	Tailpipe	5 years/100,000 km

IGNITION SYSTEM

Cable set	60,000 km	Spark plugs	20,000 km
Electronic module	5 years/100,000 km	Tune-up	20,000 km
Retiming	20,000 km		

SAFETY COMPONENTS

Airbags	life of vehicle	Stability control	5 years/100,000 km
Seat belts	life of vehicle		

STEERING AND SUSPENSION

Alignment	1 year/20,000 km	Struts	5 years/100,000 km
Ball joints	10 years/200,000 km	Tires (radial)	5 years/100,000 km
Coil springs	10 years/200,000 km	Truck tie-rod ends	5 years/100,000 km
Power steering	5 years/100,000 km	Wheel bearing	3 years/60,000 km
Shock absorber	3 years/60,000 km		

NOTE:

Many of the guidelines for the above table were extrapolated from Chrysler and Ford payouts to thousands of dissatisfied customers over the past several decades; Chrysler's original seven-year powertrain warranty (applicable 1991–95 and reapplied 2001–04); Nissan's ten-year extended powertrain warranty; Ford and GM transmission warranties outlined in their secret warranties; Ford, GM, and Toyota engine "goodwill" programs laid out in their internal service bulletins; and court judgments where judges have given their own guidelines as to what is meant by "reasonable durability."

Safety features — with the exception of anti-lock brake systems (ABS) — generally have a lifetime warranty, but airbags are a different matter. Those that are deployed in an accident —and the personal injury and interior damage their deployment will likely have caused — are covered by your accident insurance policy. However, if there is a sudden deployment for no apparent reason, the automaker and dealer should be held jointly responsible for all injuries and damages caused by the airbag. You can prove their liability by downloading data from your vehicle's data recorder. This will likely lead to a more generous settlement from the two parties and prevent your insurance premiums from being jacked up. Be sure to use both the Kravitz and Donoghue judgments in holding the dealer and carmaker responsible for costs.

PROCEDURES OF DUBIOUS VALUE

AMERICAN ACADEMY OF FAMILY PHYSICIANS

Don't do imaging for low back pain within the first six weeks, unless red flags are present. Red flags include, but are not limited to, severe or progressive neurological deficits or when serious underlying conditions such as osteomyelitis are suspected. Imaging of the lower spine before six weeks does not improve outcomes, but does increase costs. Low back pain is the fifth most common reason for all physician visits.

1. **Don't routinely prescribe antibiotics for acute mild-to-moderate sinusitis unless symptoms last for seven or more days, or symptoms worsen after initial clinical improvement.** Symptoms must include discoloured nasal secretions and facial or dental tenderness when touched. Most sinusitis in the ambulatory setting is due to a viral infection that will resolve on its own. Despite consistent recommendations to the contrary, antibiotics are prescribed in more than 80 percent of outpatient visits for acute sinusitis. Sinusitis accounts for sixteen million office visits and $5.8 billion in annual health care costs.

2. **Don't use dual-energy X-ray absorptiometry (DEXA) screening for osteoporosis in women younger than sixty-five or men younger than seventy with no risk factors.** DEXA is not cost effective in younger, low-risk patients, but is cost effective in older patients.

3. **Don't order annual electrocardiograms (EKGs) or any other cardiac screening for low-risk patients without symptoms.** There is little evidence that detection of coronary artery stenosis in asymptomatic patients at low risk for coronary heart disease improves health outcomes. False-positive tests are likely to

lead to harm through unnecessary invasive procedures, over-treatment and misdiagnosis. Potential harms of this routine annual screening exceed the potential benefit.

4. Don't perform Pap smears on women younger than twenty-one or who have had a hysterectomy for non-cancer disease. Most observed abnormalities in adolescents regress spontaneously, therefore Pap smears for this age group can lead to unnecessary anxiety, additional testing and cost. Pap smears are not helpful in women after hysterectomy (for non-cancer disease) and there is little evidence for improved outcomes.

5. Don't schedule elective, non–medically indicated inductions of labour or Cesarean deliveries before 39 weeks, 0 days gestational age. Delivery prior to 39 weeks, 0 days has been shown to be associated with an increased risk of learning disabilities and a potential increase in morbidity and mortality. There are clear medical indications for delivery prior to 39 weeks and 0 days based on maternal and/or fetal conditions. A mature fetal lung test, in the absence of appropriate clinical criteria, is not an indication for delivery.

6. Avoid elective, non–medically indicated inductions of labour between 39 weeks, 0 days and 41 weeks, 0 days unless the cervix is deemed favorable. Ideally, labour should start on its own initiative whenever possible. Higher Caesarean delivery rates result from inductions of labour when the cervix is unfavourable. Health care clinicians should discuss the risks and benefits with their patients before considering inductions of labour without medical indications.

7. Don't screen for carotid artery stenosis (CAS) in asymptomatic adult patients. There is good evidence that for adult patients with no symptoms of carotid artery stenosis, the harms of screening outweigh the benefits. Screening could lead to non-indicated surgeries that result in serious harms, including death, stroke and myocardial infarction.

8. Don't screen women older than sixty-five years of age for cervical cancer who have had adequate prior screening and are not otherwise at high risk for cervical cancer. There is adequate evidence that screening women older than sixty-five years of age for cervical cancer who have had adequate prior screening and are not otherwise at high risk provides little to no benefit.

9. Don't screen women younger than thirty years of age for cervical cancer with HPV testing, alone or in combination with cytology. There is adequate evidence that the harms of HPV testing, alone or in combination with cytology, in women younger than thirty years of age are moderate. The harms include more frequent testing and invasive diagnostic procedures such as colposcopy and cervical biopsy. Abnormal screening test results are also associated with psychological harms, anxiety and distress.

AMERICAN COLLEGE OF CARDIOLOGY

1. Don't perform stress cardiac imaging or advanced non-invasive imaging in the initial evaluation of patients without cardiac symptoms unless high-risk markers are present. Asymptomatic, low-risk patients account for up to 45 percent of unnecessary "screening." Testing should be performed only when the following findings are present: diabetes in patients older than forty, peripheral arterial disease, or greater than 2 percent yearly risk for coronary heart disease events.

2. Don't perform annual stress cardiac imaging or advanced non-invasive imaging as part of routine follow-up in asymptomatic patients. Performing stress cardiac imaging or advanced non-invasive imaging in patients without symptoms on a serial or scheduled pattern (e.g., every one to two years or at a heart procedure anniversary) rarely results in any meaningful change in patient management. This practice may, in fact, lead to unnecessary invasive procedures and excess radiation exposure without any proven impact on patients' outcomes. An exception to this rule would be for patients more than five years after a bypass operation.

3. Don't perform stress cardiac imaging or advanced non-invasive imaging as a pre-operative assessment in patients scheduled to undergo low-risk non-cardiac surgery. Non-invasive testing is not useful for patients undergoing low-risk non-cardiac surgery (e.g., cataract removal). These types of tests do not change the patient's clinical management or outcomes and will result in increased costs.

4. Don't perform echocardiography as routine follow-up for mild, asymptomatic native valve disease in adult patients with no change in signs

or symptoms. Patients with native valve disease usually have years without symptoms before the onset of deterioration. An echocardiogram is not recommended yearly unless there is a change in clinical status.

5. Don't perform stenting of non-culprit lesions during percutaneous coronary intervention (PCI) for uncomplicated hemodynamically stable ST-segment elevation myocardial infarction (STEMI). Stent placement in a noninfarct artery during primary PCI for STEMI in a hemodynamically stable patient may lead to increased mortality and complications. While potentially beneficial in patients with hemodynamic compromise, intervention beyond the culprit lesion during primary PCI has not demonstrated benefit in clinical trials to date.

AMERICAN GERIATRICS SOCIETY

1. Don't recommend percutaneous feeding tubes in patients with advanced dementia; instead offer oral assisted feeding. Careful hand-feeding for patients with severe dementia is at least as good as tube-feeding for the outcomes of death, aspiration pneumonia, functional status and patient comfort. Food is the preferred nutrient. Tube-feeding is associated with agitation, increased use of physical and chemical restraints and worsening pressure ulcers.

2. Don't use antipsychotics as first choice to treat behavioural and psychological symptoms of dementia. People with dementia often exhibit aggression, resistance to care and other challenging or disruptive behaviours. In such instances, antipsychotic medicines are often prescribed, but they provide limited benefit and can cause serious harm, including stroke and premature death. Use of these drugs should be limited to cases where non-pharmacologic measures have failed and patients pose an imminent threat to themselves or others. Identifying and addressing causes of behaviour change can make drug treatment unnecessary.

3. Avoid using medications to achieve hemoglobin A1c <7.5% in most adults age sixty-five and older; moderate control is generally better. There is no evidence that using medications to achieve tight glycemic control in older adults with type 2 diabetes is beneficial. Among non-older adults, except for long-term

reductions in myocardial infarction and mortality with metformin, using medications to achieve glycated hemoglobin levels less than 7 percent is associated with harms, including higher mortality rates. Tight control has been consistently shown to produce higher rates of hypoglycemia in older adults. Given the long timeframe to achieve theorized microvascular benefits of tight control, glycemic targets should reflect patient goals, health status, and life expectancy. Reasonable glycemic targets would be 7.0–7.5 percent in healthy older adults with long life expectancy, 7.5–8.0 percent in those with moderate comorbidity and a life expectancy less than ten years, and 8.0–9.0 percent in those with multiple morbidities and shorter life expectancy.

4. **Don't use benzodiazepines or other sedative-hypnotics in older adults as first choice for insomnia, agitation or delirium.** Large scale studies consistently show that the risk of motor vehicle accidents, falls and hip fractures leading to hospitalization and death can more than double in older adults taking benzodiazepines and other sedative-hypnotics. Older patients, their caregivers and their providers should recognize these potential harms when considering treatment strategies for insomnia, agitation or delirium. Use of benzodiazepines should be reserved for alcohol withdrawal symptoms/delirium tremens or severe generalized anxiety disorder unresponsive to other therapies.

5. **Don't use antimicrobials to treat bacteriuria in older adults unless specific urinary tract symptoms are present.** Cohort studies have found no adverse outcomes for older men or women associated with asymptomatic bacteriuria. Antimicrobial treatment studies for asymptomatic bacteriuria in older adults demonstrate no benefits and show increased adverse antimicrobial effects. Consensus criteria has been developed to characterize the specific clinical symptoms that, when associated with bacteriuria, define urinary tract infection. Screening for and treatment of asymptomatic bacteriuria is recommended before urologic procedures for which mucosal bleeding is anticipated.

Appendix D

HELPFUL INTERNET SITES

CONSUMER PROTECTION

100+1 Complaint Letters that Work
(www.scribd.com/doc/34742420/101-Complaint-Letters)

Here you will find letters that are easily copied for almost any problem that may arise. From the humourous to the threatening, these letters are both entertaining and timesaving.

Canadian Transport Agency (www.cta.gc.ca)

The Canadian Transportation Agency is an independent administrative body of the Government of Canada. It performs two key functions within the federal transportation system:

- As a quasi-judicial tribunal, informally and through formal adjudication, the agency resolves a range of commercial and consumer transportation-related disputes, including accessibility issues for persons with disabilities. It operates like a court when adjudicating disputes.

- As an economic regulator, the agency makes determinations and issues authorities, licences and permits to transportation carriers under federal jurisdiction.

Lately, the CTA has made a number of pro-consumer judgments relative to the advertising of all-in fares, the publishing of complaint numbers per airline flying in Canada, and the expansion of passenger rights. For example, CTA now says *passengers should be allowed to opt for a full refund and a free trip home if a cancellation or overbooking throws a wrench into their travel plans.* Until now, airlines have had discretion over whether to grant a refund or rebook passengers. The agency also says that in certain cases carriers must rebook passengers on the first available flight — even if that flight is with a competing airline.

Automobile Protection Association (www.apa.ca)

A motherlode of honest, independent, and current car-buying information, the non-profit APA has been protecting Canadian motorists for over forty years from its offices in Toronto and Montreal. This dynamic consumer group fights for safer vehicles for consumers and has exposed many scams associated with new-vehicle sales, leasing, and repairs. For a small fee, it will send you the invoice price for most new vehicles and help you out if you get a bad car or dealer. The APA also has a useful free online guide for digging out court judgments.

Canadian Legal Information Institute (www.canlii.org)

Be your own legal "eagle" and save big bucks. Use this site to find court judgments from every province and territory all the way up to the Supreme Court of Canada.

CBC TV's Marketplace (www.cbc.ca/marketplace)

Marketplace has been the CBC's premier national consumer show for almost forever. Staffers are dedicated to searching out scammers, airbag dangers, misleading advertising, and unsafe, poor-quality products. Search the archives for auto info, or contact the show's producers to suggest program ideas.

Class Actions in Canada (www.classproceedings.ca)

After successfully kicking Ford's rear end over its front-end thick film ignition (TFI) troubles and getting a million-dollar out-of-court settlement, this powerhouse Ontario-based law firm got a similar settlement from GM as compensation for a decade of defective V6 intake manifold gasket failures. Estimated damages were well over a billion dollars. The firm has also worked with others to force Liberty Mutual and other insurers to refund money paid by policy holders who were forced to accept accident repairs with used, reconditioned parts instead of new, original-equipment parts.

Competition Bureau Canada (www.competitionbureau.gc.ca)

The Competition Bureau is responsible for the administration and enforcement of the *Competition Act*, the *Consumer Packaging and*

Labelling Act, the *Textile Labelling Act*, and the *Precious Metals Marking Act.* Its role is to promote and maintain fair competition so that Canadians can benefit from lower prices, increased product choices, and quality services.

Most auto-related complaints submitted to the bureau concern price-fixing and misleading advertising. After *Lemon-Aid*, the APA, and Mohamed Bouchama from the ACC submitted formal complaints to Ottawa against Toyota's Access pricing program a few years ago, the automaker settled the case for $2.3 million. The bureau agreed to drop its inquiry into charges that the automaker rigged new car prices.

Almost twenty-eight years earlier, an APA complaint forced GM to pay a $20,000 fine for lying in newspaper ads, touting the Vauxhall Firenza's triumphant cross-Canada "reliability run." The cars constantly broke down, and one auto journalist brought along for the ride spilled the beans to Ottawa probers. GM took the car off the market shortly thereafter.

Consumer Affairs (www.consumeraffairs.com/automotive/manufacturers.htm)

Expecting some namby-pamby consumer affairs site? You won't find that here. It's a "seller beware" kind of website, where you'll find the scandals before they hit the mainstream press.

Consumer Reports and Consumers Union (www.consumerreports.org/cro/cars.htm)

It costs US$5.95 a month to subscribe online, but *CR*'s database is chock full of comparison tests and in-depth stories on products and services. The group's $29.95 New Car Price service is similar to what the APA offers, except for one caveat: *Consumer Reports* charges more than double the US$14 it charges American subscribers for the service. As a former Consumers Union board member, I find this practice both insulting to the magazine's loyal Canadian fans and totally unjustified when you consider that the Canadian dollar is almost at parity with the American greenback.

LawyersandSettlements.com (www.lawyersandsettlements.com)

This site covers all of the major consumer product liability litigation, class actions, and settlements in North America.

Protégez-Vous (Protect Yourself) (www.protegez-vous.qc.ca)

Quebec's French-language monthly consumer protection magazine and website is a hard-hitting critic of the auto industry. *Protégez-Vous* has supported the APA in testing dealer honesty and ratings of new and used cars in Quebec and throughout Canada. The magazine publishes dozens of test-drive results as well as articles relating to a broad range of products and services sold in Canada.

Supreme Court of Canada (scc.lexum.umontreal.ca/en/index.html)

It's not enough to have a solid claim against a company or the government. Supporting your position with a Supreme Court decision also helps. Three pro-consumer judgments rendered in February 2002 are particularly useful:

- *Bannon v. Thunder Bay (City):* An injured resident missed the deadline to file a claim against Thunder Bay; however, the Supreme Court maintained that extenuating factors, such as being under the effects of medication, extended her time to file. A good case to remember next time your vehicle is damaged by a pothole or you are injured by a municipality's negligence.

- *R. v. Guignard:* This judgment says you can protest as long as you speak or write the truth and you don't disturb the peace or harass customers or workers.

- *Whiten v. Pilot Insurance Co.:* The insured's home burned down, and the insurance company refused to pay the claim. The jury was outraged and ordered the company to pay the $345,000 claim, plus $320,000 for legal costs and $1 million in punitive damages, making it the largest punitive damage award in Canadian history. The Supreme Court maintained the jury's decision, calling Pilot "the insurer from hell." This judgment scares the dickens out of insurers, who fear that they might face huge punitive damage awards if they don't pay promptly.

AUTO SAFETY

Center for Auto Safety (www.autosafety.org)

A Ralph Nader–founded agency that provides free online info on model-specific safety- and performance-related defects.

Crashtest.com (www.crashtest.com)

This website has crash-test information from around the world. You can find additional crashworthiness data for cars just recently coming on to the North American market that have been sold for many years in Asia, Europe, or Australia. The Honda Fit (Jazz), Mercedes Smart, Magna's Opel lineup, and Ford's upcoming European Fiesta and Focus imports are just a few examples.

Insurance Institute for Highway Safety (www.iihs.org)

A dazzling site that's long on crash photos and graphs that show which vehicles are the most crashworthy in side and offset collisions and which head restraints work best.

SafetyForum (www.safetyforum.com)

The Forum contains comprehensive news archives and links to useful sites, plus names of court-recognized experts on everything from unsafe Chrysler minivan latches to dangerous van conversions.

Transport Canada (www.tc.gc.ca/eng/roadsafety/safevehicles-defectinvestigations-index-76.htm)

A ho-hum site that's in no way as informative as the NHTSA or IIHS sites. You can access recalls for 1970–2010 models, but owner complaints aren't listed, defect investigations aren't disclosed, and service bulletin summaries aren't provided. A list of used vehicles admissible for import is available at *www.tc.gc.ca/roadsafety/safe vehicles/importation/usa/vafus/list2/menu.htm* or by calling the Registrar of Imported Vehicles (RIV) at 1-888-848-8240.

U.S. National Highway Traffic Safety Administration (www.safercar.gov)

This site has a comprehensive free database covering owner complaints, recall campaigns, crashworthiness and rollover ratings, defect investigations, service bulletin summaries, and safety research papers.

MEDIATION/PROTEST

Ontario Ministry of Consumer Affairs (www.sse.gov.on.ca/mcs/Documents/complaint_not.pdf)

Any complaint that is even remotely covered by provincial consumer protection legislation should be copied online to this provincial government agency.

Canadian Competition Bureau (www.competitionbureau.gc.ca/eic/site/cb-bc.
nsf/frm-eng/GH%C3%89T-7TDNA5)

Another site that will get the government involved. After posting your grievance online, federal government investigators will look into complaints relative to misleading advertising, price-fixing, etc.

Service Canada (www.servicecanada.gc.ca/eng/ocs)

Ticked off about government indifference? Looking for that pension cheque? Here is where Ottawa takes your online complaint about — Ottawa.

Information/Services

Alberta Government's Vehicle Cost Calculator (www.agric.gov.ab.ca/app24/
costcalculators/vehicle/getvechimpls.jsp)

Your tax dollars at work. This handy calculator allows you to estimate and compare the ownership and operating costs for any business or non-business vehicles. Eleven types of vehicles can be compared and the ownership cost can be calculated by modifying the input values. Alternatively, you may select the same model if you wish to compare one vehicle but with variations in purchase price, options, fuel type (diesel or gas), interest rates, or length of ownership.

ALLDATA Service Bulletins (www.alldata.com/recalls/index.html)

Free summaries of automotive recalls and technical service bulletins are listed by year, make, model, and engine option. You can access your vehicle's full bulletins online by paying a $26.95 (U.S.) subscription fee.

BMJ Quality & Safety (qualitysafety.bmj.com)

An international peer review publication providing, news, opinion, debate and research for academics, clinicians and healthcare managers. It encourages innovation and creative thinking to improve the quality of health care and the science of improvement.

Complaints Board (www.complaintsboard.com/bycountry/canada.html)

If you scroll down on this site you'll see that even Tim Horton's has a few unhappy customers.

Healthy Weight (ww.healthyweight.net/fraud1.html)

A tough, no-nonsense site that peels away the layers of false information about diets and good health.

International Cruise Victims (www.internationalcruisevictims.org/LatestMemberStories/Member_Stories_Categories.html)

Essentially a compendium of cruise ship travellers' experiences on the "dark side" of cruising.

Kelley Blue Book and Edmunds (www.kbb.com; www.edmunds.com)

Prices and technical info are American-oriented, but you'll find good reviews of almost every vehicle sold in North America — plus there's an informative readers' forum.

Online Metric Conversions (www.sciencemadesimple.net/conversions.html)

A great place to instantly convert gallons to litres, miles to kilometres, etc., and for cruise ship passengers, nautical miles to — the next buffet.

Tuum est, or "It's up to You" (www.tuum-est.com)

This website outlines the legal rights of the physically disabled and gives useful tips on pleading your own medical malpractice lawsuits. Extensive links to courts, jurisprudence, and other groups are especially helpful.

Women's Garage (www.womensgarage.com)

Yes, women are wired differently. No razzle-dazzle on this site. Just straightforward information on getting the best repairs for the least amount of money and tips on spotting incompetent mechanics, before your car is up on the hoist.